THE ART AND TECHNIQUE OF PAINTING ON PORCELAIN

GEORGES MISEREZ-SCHIRA

THE ART AND TECHNIQUE OF PAINTING ON PORCELAIN

Translated by Camilla Sykes

Patrick Stephens, Cambridge

Copyright © 1974 by Edita S.A., Lausanne
Published in Great Britain in 1974 by Patrick Stephens Limited
Bar Hill, Cambridge, CB3 8EL

All rights reserved. No part of this publication may be reproduced, stored in a retrieval system, or transmitted, in any form or by any means, electronic, mechanical, photocopying, recording or otherwise, without prior permission of the publishers.

Printed in Switzerland

ISBN 0 85059 189 9

I dedicate this work to my late wife,
a true artist and,
to me, a most wonderful teacher.

CREATED AND PRODUCED
BY
EDITA LAUSANNE

CONTENTS

PUBLISHER'S FOREWORD

The object of this book is a practical one: to put an approved method of decorating china and earthenware within everybody's reach. The book appears at a timely moment: industrialisation has suppressed the craftsman-decorator, but the greater leisure of today has encouraged new activities, in particular that of painting on porcelain. The decorators of the past have disappeared: only a few rare professionals have preserved their method and the secrets of their trade, but these professionals are virtually unknown to the enthusiasts of today. It is in order to fill this gap that we have called upon a workshop which has perpetuated the traditions of this craft and at the same time adapted itself to the technical and social demands of our time.

The method recommended by Georges Miserez-Schira is the fruit of a profound knowledge of this craft and of long experience in teaching the art of painting on porcelain. The amateur will find all the necessary information here. However, these helpful recipes will be ineffective unless accompanied by constant practice, which is essential to the acquisition of a supple touch with the paint-brush and to the development of a sense of design. Once the hesitations of the beginner have been overcome, painting on porcelain will be a joyful experience. The first successful and attractive object made will be the source of legitimate pride.

The numerous examples of decoration in this book have been chosen to serve as stepping-stones to imagination and sensibility: they will help beginners, stimulate amateurs and arouse new enthusiasm for the art of painting on porcelain.

A SHORT HISTORY OF CERAMICS

THE BIRTH OF AN ART AND ITS FIRST DEVELOPMENTS

Historians have found some difficulty in determining the precise moment when ceramics first appeared. Ceramics do, however, indicate an important stage in the evolution of peoples and are a characteristic product of a sedentary population, for two reasons: first of all, the potter cannot transport his wheel, however rudimentary it may be, nor his kiln nor the clay he uses; secondly, pottery is too fragile to withstand the jolts of the nomadic life whereas it is of practical use to a sedentary people.

But although the date of the first appearance of ceramics is not known, its areas of origin are, and these are on the sites of the first agricultural settlements, in the valleys of the Nile, the Tigris and Euphrates, the Indus and the Yellow River. How can we explain the fact that, in both simultaneous and different ages, among civilisations having no contact with each other and in far-removed continents, man should have come to the astonishing conclusion that a marly substance of varying colour, which is fairly easily adapted to the fashioning of utilitarian, decorative or votive objects should, on contact with fire, be transformed into a hard, resonant, weather-resisting material?

Naturally, there are several reasonably convincing answers to this question. The most plausible is probably this: when making a fire on clay soil, man noticed that the earth remained hard-baked after heavy rain, whereas his footprints remained in the sticky clay all round the fire. The first objects fashioned by man were thus destined for domestic use and it is logical to assume that these bowls or cups were modelled to resemble plants or fruit, gourds or marrows. Archaic periods in every civilisation provide quantities of examples showing the skill and even the aesthetic sense of the first potters.

It is perhaps interesting to note that although the potter's wheel was used in Egypt as early as the first Pharaonic age, in archaic Greece as mentioned by Homer, and in China 2,500 years BC, it never appeared in the ancient American civilisations.

The decoration of primitive ceramics was limited to incisions with rudimentary tools or to pressure with the fingers. The first colour decoration was obtained from the application of slip, a clayey substance containing iron oxide dye, which produced beiges, ochres, browns and blacks.

But soon a new discovery intervened, that of glazing or applying a kind of glass paste. Its discovery must have come about in the same way as that of clay. Alkaline ash combined with the siliceous soil and transformed it into a transparent substance through the action of the fire, and the result was glass. The need to obtain waterproof ceramics led the potter to cover his vases with a layer of vitrifiable material, and faience was born. Of course the potter made very varied use of this discovery before achieving the refined product which we know today, which is the result of many centuries of research.

ANTIQUITY

In Egypt the first glazed pottery had already made its appearance during the pre-historic era. The Egyptians have produced ceramics throughout their history, but one remembers especially the intense turquoise blue which covers pottery made from a fine siliceous white clay. On this blue ground the ornamentation—hieroglyphs, symbols etc.—was obtained by means of black enamel set into the hollows of the incised decoration.

The Chaldeans and the Assyrians, by using brick in preference to stone, adopted ceramics as the principal element of their architecture. Babylonian art blazes out in sumptuously decorated walls of glazed brick, such as the frieze of archers in the palace of Artaxerxes of the fifth century BC at Susa. This flowering of glazed brickwork continued into Moslem times.

A brilliant civilisation, corresponding to the last three millennia before the Christian era, developed along the shores of the Aegean Sea. Its rather crude pottery may be considered as the first efforts of European ceramics. The art gradually became more refined and the excavations carried out on the island of Crete, at Knossos and Phaestos, have yielded an abundance of very original pottery. The vases are made on the potter's wheel and their naturalistic decoration is inspired by the flora and marine fauna of the region. After a period of magnificent expansion, the Mycenean civilisation fell into decay at the end of the Bronze Age. From the ninth to the eighth century BC geometrical decoration became general throughout Greece. Attica then became the principal centre for the production of ceramics. The complicated decoration of the Greeks—linear motifs, rosettes etc.—is obtained by means of a shiny black vitrified varnish applied directly on to the red clay.

The influence of the East, acquired through constant commercial exchange, can be noticed, especially in the islands of Crete and Cyprus, which have provided wonderful examples. Towards the middle of the sixth century under the influence of Athens a new kind of ceramic appears, free from both the geometrical and the oriental traditions. Although the technique has hardly changed—black patterns on a red ground, or red on black—the decoration is more refined and the Greek painters show considerable mastery of design. Mythological or anecdotal subjects precisely illustrate the life of ancient times in its most diverse forms. In contrast to the rich inventiveness of the designs the colour scale is still limited: red and black, both obtained from iron ore, form the basis to which is sometimes added a background of milky white. Highlights of blue and purplish red are the only accents among these basic colours. Thanks to the enterprising spirit of these people, the enormous output of the Greek potters was used as barter and exported to all the Mediterranean countries and even to South Russia, where this pottery was valued as much for its contents of wine and oil as for its use as containers.

In Italy the Etruscans and afterwards the Romans produced beautiful red pottery decorated in relief, known as sigillate pottery, which became more and more elaborate as it became less utilitarian.

Etruscan vase of the eighth to seventh century BC (above, right). — This vase of brown clay derives its shape from a water-skin; the long spout ends in a bull's head. On top is a warrior on horseback wearing a crested helmet, a round shield slung across his shoulders.

Ceramic cup from Athens, fourth century BC (above). — With limited means at their disposal the Athenian potters managed to decorate their work with countless scenes from mythology or from daily life. Here, a woman musician plays the double flute to delight the ear of a music lover.

The frieze of archers at Susa, fifth century BC. — This famous frieze is made from an assemblage of glazed bricks; the figures in light relief are shown marching along the full length of the wall of Artaxerxes' palace.

THE FAR EAST

The oldest Chinese ceramics date from the second millennium BC. Towards the end of the Chou dynasty in the 5th century BC the Chinese, by experimenting with the reaction of certain clays to high temperatures, were able to produce the first stoneware, a vitrified material which was both waterproof and very resistant.
The ceramics produced during the Han dynasty, from 206 BC to 220 AD, were almost exclusively of a funerary nature. In much of the stoneware of this period there is already a proportion of china-clay, the forerunner of porcelain, which was soon to follow.
Four centuries of anarchy succeeded the Han dynasty. During the next two dynasties (the Sui 589-618 AD and the Tang 618-907 AD) the influence of sculptors on clay modellers was considerable. A number of small figures have survived from this period; they have undeniable charm, representing people and horses decorated in shiny glazes and brilliant colours. It is the most ostentatious period of Chinese ceramics. During the Sung dynasty ceramics continued to maintain a very high standard: particularly noteworthy is the 'celadon' ware, which was so successful in its own time that it was exported in quantity to Japan and Western Asia.
Towards the beginning of the fourteenth century a new technique appeared which was to have important repercussions in ceramic art, that of the blue under-glaze. This kind of decoration is the origin of Delft pottery, in which European ceramic artists strove to imitate this highly prized Chinese ware.
The Ching dynasty which succeeded the Ming marked an age of ever increasing prosperity. In the reign of K'ang-hsi (1662-1722) the production was extremely varied: we should note in particular the famous *famille verte* with its rich decoration, and also the monochrome glazes such as *sang-de-bœuf, fouetté, soufflé, foie-de-mulet* etc. In order to please the taste of European importers the Chinese went so far as to imitate certain Japanese wares which were much in demand, such as Imari ware with its cobalt blue under-glaze and copper-red decoration picked out in gold, made by the easily-fired method.
Famille rose china appears in the reign of Yung Cheng: the dominant purplish pink of European origin imparts a delicate quality to this porcelain. We should also note the egg-shell glazes, which are marvels of technique.
This technical virtuosity became more accentuated in the reign of K'ien Lung (1736-1796) but unfortunately it was often at the expense of artistic merit. The decoration became heavier, and the enormous output of the whole eighteenth century was almost entirely absorbed by the Compagnie des Indes. This china was made for the export market and decorated according to the taste of a European clientele, with armorial bearings, portraits, seascapes etc.
From the beginning of the reign of K'ien Lung and throughout the nineteenth century, the vast ceramic output of China consisted of more or less skilful repetitions of the old designs.
Japanese ceramics followed an almost parallel course although the decoration was unmistakably different from the Chinese. Japanese master potters were excellent in the making of stoneware, but the Chinese were indisputably the greatest makers of porcelain.

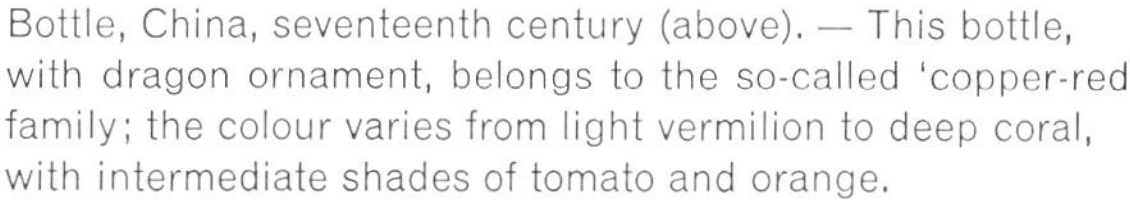

Bottle, China, seventeenth century (above). — This bottle, with dragon ornament, belongs to the so-called 'copper-red' family; the colour varies from light vermilion to deep coral, with intermediate shades of tomato and orange.

Plate, China, eighteenth century (above, right). — An example of 'famille rose', this plate has the characteristic 'seven-border' decoration, showing the skill of Chinese painters.

Vase, China, eighteenth century (right). — This pot-bellied vase also belongs to the 'famille rose' and is decorated with hundreds of flowers; the detailed illustration (below) shows the richness and skill of the stylisation.

Jug, Iznik, sixteenth century. — This pottery has considerable charm, with its stylised floral decoration on a red ground.

Bowl, Persia, seventeenth century (bottom). — Persian potters succeeded in producing faience with under-glaze decoration which almost rivals Chinese porcelain.

Dish, Ray (Iran), thirteenth century (below). — Through different stages of firing, seven colours have been applied under and over an ivory glaze—blue, purple, green, black, red, white and brown.

ISLAM

Moslem ceramics form an essential link between Far Eastern porcelain and European faience.

It is impossible to say for certain which were the centres of production. The most important factor is that various sovereigns attracted the best artisans to their courts from different parts of Islam: the result was a mixture of traditions difficult to identify with any precision.

All the Moslem countries produced great quantities of ceramics. The most ancient pieces have been found in Iran, but it is not certain that they were made on the spot. Ninth and tenth century objects originating from the borders of Turkestan and found along the famous silk route show the influence of Chinese art of the T'ang period. Later on, Persian pottery developed its characteristic decoration of figures, arabesques and floral motifs on ivory or deep blue grounds. In Iraq, pottery was enriched through the discovery of an original process which was probably perfected at Samara in the ninth century: this was the metallic lustre obtained by a second firing with oxides of copper and silver superimposed on a glazed ground. This technique continued to be used later, especially by Spanish ceramicists, and suffuses the object with a lustre which is comparable to the glitter of gold ornaments.

In Egypt, from the tenth to the twelfth century under the Fatimids, local artists produced pieces with light airy decoration covered in a golden yellow lustre of fine quality, which was made according to the process perfected at Samara. Among the most frequently used themes, long-eared quadrupeds are to be found on a background of foliage; and there are characters bearing Christian emblems, which show Coptic influence and are evidence of the climate of tolerance to be found in the country at that time.

With the arrival of the Turks from Central Asia, the use of ceramics as architectural decoration for public and religious monuments developed. Mosques were ornamented with marvellous panels in which blues and blacks predominated. Flowers were the most important decorative element; roses, carnations, poppies and peonies are vigorously portrayed.

In Persia, under the Sefevids from the sixteenth to the beginning of the eighteenth century, the favourite themes are gardens, court life and everyday scenes, which seem to step straight out of a Persian miniature.

In the Middle East during the sixteenth century the Ottomans developed a kind of pottery which was greatly appreciated in Europe. At first blue on a white ground, the decoration was later embellished with turquoise blue, lime green and aubergine purple. Ottoman pottery reached its highest point in the middle of the sixteenth century with the introduction of tomato red; large bunches of the four classical flowers—peonies, poppies, roses and carnations—were very freely drawn and, in Iznik pottery, they mingled with the lotus and cloud patterns of the Chinese.

North Africa, particularly Tunisia, had its own kind of pottery in the seventeenth century, which can be seen in all its beauty in the famous mosque of the Berbers at Kairouan.

Moslem potters never learned the secret of making porcelain; they devoted all their talent to the production of glazed pottery and faience.

A SHORT HISTORY OF FAIENCE AND PORCELAIN IN EUROPE

During the Middle Ages Europeans produced pottery which was rustic and utilitarian. In the fifteenth century faience gained the place of honour in Italy, at Florence with Luca della Robbia and at Urbino, Pesaro, Deruta, Gubbio and of course at Faenza, where the word 'faience' originated. As the taste for Italian art was general in Europe at that time, the French and Dutch lost no time in copying Italian faience.

The great rise of faience in France dates from the seventeenth century; the principal centres were then at Nevers, Rouen and Moustiers, where the manufacture of hard-fired wares was carried out, in imitation of the Italians. In the second half of the eighteenth century the technique of soft-firing (1300 to 1450 degrees Fahrenheit) developed, and was responsible for the growing success of the potters of Marseilles, Strasbourg and Sceaux. Thanks to this new technique, the palette was enriched by a whole new scale of colours.

Faience was equally successful in other countries of Europe: at Delft in Holland; at Hanau, Nuremberg, Höchst and Ansbach in Germany; and at Alcora, Malaga and Marisès in Spain. Faience remained as the highlight of ceramic production until it was ousted by the invasion of porcelain from China through the intermediary of the Compagnie des Indes, causing the decline of the faience workshops. Only local or regional centres were able to survive, by continuing to produce objects of utilitarian nature and in peasant style, some of which are greatly appreciated today. German ceramicists excelled in the production of stoneware, which was often imitated.

In England, the evolution of ceramics was different from that of the continent. As pottery had developed very slowly in England up till the seventeenth century, faience was imported from Delft. In 1720 John Astbury, the son of a Burslem potter, had the idea of mixing silicate powder with his clay, an invention which was the origin of English china.

Chinese porcelain had inspired Europeans with enthusiasm when it first came to Europe in the sixteenth century because of its purity and whiteness. For over two centuries European craftsmen sought the secret of hard-paste porcelain in vain. In 1709 Johann Friedrich Böttger, a German chemist who was the protégé of the Prince-Elector of Saxony, succeeded in making hard-paste porcelain for the first time in Europe. Frederick Augustus II of Saxony built the workshop at Meissen which was the original manufacturing centre for the china of this name. But Meissen was unable to keep the secret of porcelain manufacturing: many other production centres were founded—in Austria at Vienna; at Höchst, Frankenthal, and Nymphenburg in Germany; at Doccia in Italy, and elsewhere in Europe. In 1761 the Sèvres workshop bought the secret of hard-paste china from Peter Anton Hannong. After the discovery of a deposit of china-clay at Saint Yrieix near Limoges, the Sèvres workshop became in its turn famous throughout Europe. Other factories were established at Limoges, Bayeux, Chantilly and Vierzon.

Porcelain had set out on the conquest of Europe: it was a total success.

Ring-shaped bottle, Lower Austria, about 1800 (above, left). — This white majolica is decorated with flowers and burlesque figures.

Covered tureen, Nyon, eighteenth century (below). — This piece, very French in feeling, is ornamented with stylised naturalistic motifs arranged in a graceful scroll pattern.

Dish, Ostergötland, 1785 (above, centre). — This Scandinavian faience is an excellent example of stylised motifs borrowed from nature. The colours are green, yellow and red.

Pot with pewter lid; Freiberg, Saxony, seventeenth century (above, right). — This salt-glazed stoneware with lattice decoration is enamelled in various colours.

Dish, Faenza, fifteenth century (opposite, above). — This magnificent faience represents the episodes of the Passion of Jesus Christ in symbolic fashion. The drawing is very simple and the colours are of a very great sobriety.

Water jug and basin, Moustiers, eighteenth century (opposite, below). — This Provençal faience represents the myth of Orpheus charming the beasts. The subject is given a natural landscape background framed in flowers, which imparts a poetic feeling compatible with the legend.

• FAIENCE AND STONEWARE CENTRES OF EUROPE

Egypt, Crete and Greece did not produce faience but the Babylonians and the Arabs did, and the Arabs brought it with them to North Africa and ultimately to Spain.

SPANISH CENTRES

The original name for faience derives from the principal workshops of the Balearic Isles, at Majorca; this gave rise to the word 'majolica'. The Hispano-Moresque workshops of Grenada produced majolica with a metallic glaze, and these coppery glints earned it the name of 'golden ware'. After the fall of the Moslem kingdom of Spain, the workshops of Paterna and Manisès and their offshoots at Toledo, Talavera and Barcelona continued to produce majolica.

ITALIAN CENTRES

In the fifteenth century, thanks to Luca della Robbia, Italy became the second home of majolica, which was supplanted by faience from Faenza. Italian centres were at Urbino, Gubbio, Deruta and especially Faenza.

FRENCH CENTRES

French centres were numerous and sometimes ephemeral. They were at the following places—
Nîmes: produced vases with portrait medallions on a blue ground.
Nevers: this workshop was active from about 1610 and its production was orientated in two different directions; one followed the taste of the time, the other favoured skilfully decorated objects with popular appeal.
Rouen: this workshop was founded in 1644 by Edme Poterat. It was mainly noted for a 'lambrequin' decoration produced in about 1700. Rouen lost its supremacy by trying to imitate Strasbourg's soft-fired decorations. Satellite workshops of Rouen were at Sinceny, Orleans, Moulins, Quimper, Le Croisic, Rennes and Saint-Cloud.
Moustiers: being close to the Italian border, the people of Moustiers in Provence at first imitated the Italians, but after 1709 they created an original kind of decoration by using the grotesque designs of Berain and Callot.
Strasbourg: in 1721, at Strasbourg, Carl Franz Hannong produced soft-fired faience in imitation of the hard-fired products of Rouen, but with a limited colour range. Later, he created the 'flowers of India' pattern, and then his original decoration 'flowers of nature'. The Strasbourg workshop became extinct in 1779. Other centres, at Niderviller, Aprey, Luneville, Holitsch in Hungary, Bayreuth and Stralsund in Germany, Rörstrand and Marieberg in Scandinavia, were all inspired by the Strasbourg workshop.
Marseilles: from 1749 Marseilles competed with Moustiers and produced a very luminous green which enjoyed a lively success until the time of the Revolution.

GERMAN CENTRES

Faience penetrated the Holy Roman Empire via Venice towards 1626; the production of tiles for the casing of stoves was quickly established. By the middle of the eighteenth century the workshops of Hanau, Frankfurt, Nuremberg, Bayreuth, Ansbach, Dresden and Berlin were making faience which was a reasonably good imitation of the Chinese. The influence of enamellers on glass was evident in the decoration of faience, often resulting in polychrome motifs of extraordinary subtlety. Later still, French influence from Strasbourg and Marseilles inspired decorators to paint flowers and modellers to try out new shapes, thereby introducing the rococo.

INRI

Delft tile, eighteenth century (above). — The potters of Delft made their faience tiles known far beyond the frontiers of their own country; these were decorated with flowers and seascapes.

◁ Water urn and basin, Saint-Omer, eighteenth century (opposite). — Birds and foliage enliven these two pieces of faience, giving them an air of rustic gaiety.

Tulip vase, Delft, eighteenth century (above, left). — A faience vase specially designed to display the characteristic flowers of the country.

From the Holy Roman Empire faience spread to to Copenhagen in Denmark, Rörstrand in Sweden and Herreböe in Norway.

DUTCH AND BELGIAN CENTRES

Faience was introduced to Antwerp by an Italian immigrant, and soon Rotterdam and Haarlem were producing tiles decorated with stylised naturalistic motifs of animals, flowers and fruit. The biggest centre was Delft, which exported its faience all over Europe. The motifs of Delft wares were at first inspired by Chinese porcelain, then by the Bible and by scenes from the everyday life of the country. The workshops of Delft disappeared in 1794, but a few centres producing this ware survive today in Holland, notably in Friesland.

CENTRES IN GREAT BRITAIN

The earliest type of majolica produced in England dates from 1601. About twenty years later, factories appeared in London, Bristol, Liverpool, Glasgow, Dublin and other places which imitated the products of Delft.

GERMAN AND ENGLISH STONEWARE

In about 1540, Rhenish potters became known for their large, pot-bellied, narrow-necked pitchers, designed for the transport of wine to England. Certain centres as, for instance, Siegburg near Bonn, also produced white stoneware; in the Westerwald, at Höhr and Grenzhausen, stoneware was always grey.

Later, Bavarian potters made chocolate-brown stoneware decorated in brilliant colours in the style of the enamelled glass of the time. Other centres were at Altenburg in Saxony and Bunzlau in Silesia.

The importing of German stoneware into England encouraged the establishment of indigenous potteries, at Oxford, Chesterfield and Swinton.

The foremost English ceramicist was Josiah Wedgwood (1730-1795): he was a first-rate craftsman who invented a cream-coloured stoneware and a fine thin stoneware called 'Queen's Ware', which made him famous. He gave his name to the factory which is still active today.

Teapot, Kassel, eighteenth century (opposite page). — Bulbous but elegant, this teapot is ornamented with flowers and scenes from daily life, a form of decoration popular at the time. It is mounted in silver gilt.

• PORCELAIN CENTRES OF EUROPE

GERMANY AND AUSTRIA

Meissen: this centre was the cradle of European porcelain in the eighteenth century, and its factory is still active today. The first designs were inspired by Chinese motifs but soon became more original, with bunches of flowers and patterns in the French manner. Meissen started the fashion for small statues and china figurines, with which it made its reputation. The factory has now been nationalized.

There were many absconders from Meissen who carried the secrets of its processes far afield, the most famous of whom was Joseph Jacob Ringler. It is to him that many German factories owe their existence and their inspiration; Höchst, Nymphenburg and Ludwigsburg being among them.

Vienna: this factory was the private property of its founder, Innocent-Claude Du Paquier, from 1718-1744; but on his death it became Imperial property. Absconders from Meissen helped to start it; the height of its fame was during the second half of the eighteenth century but its decline had already begun in the first years of the nineteenth. China decorated in relief, with great variety of design in which copper-red, purple and green predominate, is the most characteristic product of this factory.

Höchst: the workshop started making faience in 1746 but changed to porcelain in 1750, thanks to the arrival of Joseph Jacob Ringler. Its history was disturbed and its activity ceased completely during the French Revolution and Napoleonic wars. Höchst owes its fame to Johann Peter Melchior, who created over 300 different models.

Fürstenberg: this workshop, like the one at Meissen, still occupies the same building which gave it birth, in this case the castle of Fürstenberg near Höxter. During the eighteenth century it had a history of many ups and downs, with commercial and financial difficulties; but happier times came with the nineteenth century. Fürstenberg never achieved the fame of Meissen, but its decorated china is particularly beautiful and its figurines are often skilfully modelled.

Berlin: this china factory owes its existence to Frederick the Great's interest in porcelain. The Berlin factory was at first privately owned but in time it became royal property. It profited by the King of Prussia's military undertakings, one of which led to the occupation of Meissen where he was able to carry out a thorough reconnaissance of the method of production. In Berlin as elsewhere, a number of well-known artists and artisans from other workshops were assembled. Although the Berlin factory went through many vicissitudes, it remained a prestige factory as long as Frederick was alive and subsequent alterations enabled its production to be industrialized, and it is still operating successfully today.

Frankenthal: Paul Anton Hannong of Strasbourg founded this factory in 1755: it had a relatively short existence of 45 years. Frankenthal was able to compete with Meissen thanks to the variety of the shapes and designs of its wares.

Ludwigsburg: founded by order of Count Carl-Eugen of Wurtemberg, this factory flourished under the learned Joseph Jacob Ringler. Ludwigsburg had its problems like all the other centres: the instability of its labour force was amazing, and many artists and artisans frequently changed their jobs in order to earn a few extra ducats.

Porringer and tray, Sèvres, eighteenth century (opposite, above). — These two pieces are probably among the first works executed in hard-paste by the Sèvres factory. They are decorated with seascapes bordered in gold; the effect is most attractive.

Dish, Meissen, eighteenth century (opposite, below). — The Meissen craftsman was inspired by the French painter Watteau when decorating this dish; the painting brilliantly portrays the shimmer of silk dresses.

Coffee-pot, Nymphenburg, eighteenth century (right). — Roses and tulipes curl round the bulge of this coffee-pot and give it a distinctly unaffected look which suits it perfectly.

Ludwigsburg porcelain never had the whiteness of Meissen, but the shapes, decoration and colours were equal to those of any other workshop. This factory ceased all activity in 1824.

Nymphenburg: as every prince had to have his own china factory, Prince Maximilian Joseph III of Bavaria presented one to his young wife Mary-Ann-Sophia, daughter of the Elector of Saxony and King of Poland. The factory started at Neudeck near Munich and was later moved to Nymphenburg, where today it still occupies the same buildings as it did two hundred years ago. Nymphenburg produced one of the greatest artists of the eighteenth century, Franz Anton Bustelli, whose figurines are famous. Today's wares are made from the old moulds and from models which have been adapted to conform with contemporary taste.

There were also other factories of lesser importance in Germany which were sometimes just as ephemeral as some of the ones mentioned above. These were at Ansbach, Kelsterbach, Fulda, Kassel, Würzburg, Gotha, Volkstedt, Rudolfstadt, Kloster-Veilsdorf and Wallendorf-Limbach. In Switzerland, the factories at Zurich and Nyon had successful careers for a few years.

FRANCE

There is one characteristic common to all French china factories: they produced hardly any hard-paste porcelain before 1772. The decisive event in this respect was the discovery of china-clay deposits at Saint-Yrieix, near Limoges.

Rouen: here was the first French porcelain factory, which was active from 1673 to 1696. Rouen porcelain is painted in cobalt blue in the same style as the Rouen faience of the time, and is rare.

Saint-Cloud: this factory, founded in 1677, produced soft-paste porcelain in series, nearly always painted in blue. It closed down in 1766.

Chantilly: produced soft-paste porcelain, of mainly utilitarian character, from 1725 onwards.

Mennecy: founded in 1748, this workshop mainly produced figurines, and china of new and original shapes with flower decoration which is often effective and beautiful.

Vincennes-Sèvres: the 'Royal Porcelain Factory of France' was a serious rival to Meissen; it started at Vincennes and moved to Sèvres in 1753. It was run as a private concern until 1759, when it became crown property; today it is still owned by the State.

Sèvres produced hard-paste porcelain in 1768-9, thanks to the discovery of china-clay at Saint-Yrieix. The Sèvres factory became famous, as much for the technical excellence of its products as for the spirit of invention and the skill of its artists and decorators. Orders flowed in from every court in Europe.

In Paris itself factories appeared which were

Coffee-pot, Meissen, eighteenth century (left). — This famous German factory started the fashion for subjects taken from everyday life: here, some miners are seen in a landscape.

Plate, Meissen, eighteenth century (opposite, top). — This is part of a whole service bearing the arms of Count Ferrero; the naturalistic decoration has a trompe-l'œil effect because each subject has its shadow. This kind of decoration was taken from natural history illustrations.

Covered pot, Vienna, eigtheenth century (opposite, below). — In this piece there is a return to the Chinese style of flower decoration, notably in the modelling of the peonies. The colours are copper-red, violet-purple, a little green, some yellow, and blue.

Breakfast set, Sèvres, eighteenth century (below). — A magnificent 'solitaire' (or 'cabaret') of four pieces with a ground of deep blue, pale blue and white 'partridge-eye' pattern, with flowers and fruit in medallions. The gilding highlights these pieces with great richness.

◁ On the opposite page several pieces of a service from Doccia (1735-1757) are shown. The characteristic motifs are inspired by botany, with occasional signs of Asiatic influence in the stylisation and disposition. The colours are mainly copper-red and green, with some shades of blue: very little gold was used at Doccia.

Dish, Worcester, c. 1765 (right). — This dish from the Worcester factory is imitated from the Japanese. The decoration is known as Imari and is a blue under-glaze painted afterwards with a rich pattern in red and gold.

patronised by Marie-Antoinette and other members of the royal family, in particular those of the rue de Thiroux, rue des Boulets, and rue de Bondy. They all disappeared during the Revolution and today their products are known as Paris porcelain. Other French factories, at Rouen, Niderviller, Limoges and Strasbourg could not compete with Sèvres, and their product is not of comparable interest.

ITALY

The first Italian porcelain factory was founded in 1720 in Venice by Francesco Vezzi. During the seven years of its existence it produced porcelain of a wonderful translucence. An original feature of these pieces is the coat-of-arms of the customer engraved in the paste or painted on the porcelain; this china is very rare. Another Venetian factory was that of Geminiano Cozzi: it was more important than Vezzi's and had a longer life, only coming to an end at the beginning of the nineteenth century. Its main products were dinner services and figurines.

The most important of all the Italian factories was at Doccia: it is still active there today. It had a slow and difficult start. Its most typical and most easily recognisable shapes are receptacles with elongated spouts and upturned nozzles in the shape of a snake's head. The decorative themes of Doccia were always very varied and very rich: biblical or pagan scenes, characters from Italian comedy, town criers and so on.

In 1738 Amalia Christina, daughter of Augustus II Elector of Saxony and King of Poland, presented her husband Charles III King of Naples with seventeen different Meissen services. Charles III was passionately interested in china and it was he who founded the factory at Capodimonte, in some buildings near his castle. This factory had only a brief existence, from 1743 to 1759, but it

Plate, Copenhagen, eighteenth century (left). — This piece is part of a service made for Catherine the Great. The book 'Flora Danica' by the learned botanist Sibthorp served as a model and gave its name to this famous set. This plate is decorated with a spray of camomile.

produced some pieces of remarkably fine quality. When he became King of Spain Charles III transported his china factory—in three ships, with forty-four workmen and their families and eighty-eight tons of material—to Buen Retiro, near Madrid. Giuseppe Gricci was the most remarkable of the artists of Capodimonte and Buen Retiro. The factory of Buen Retiro ceased all activity in 1808.

ENGLAND

English porcelain was inspired by Chinese and Japanese, French and German pieces. The oldest English factory is that of Chelsea, which produced characteristic small scent-bottles in the shape of toys. The Derby factory later absorbed Chelsea and produced every kind of article which could be made from china, and continued production until 1848. Other English factories, at Bow and Bristol, had only a short existence, due to financial difficulties.

DENMARK

The Copenhagen factory, founded in 1760, still operates today and has always produced a great deal of table ware. Its most famous service is called 'Flora Danica' and was made for Catherine the Great. It consists of 1335 pieces, 632 of which compose the breakfast set.

HOLLAND

In this country the factories at Weesp, Oude-Loosdrecht and The Hague, although they had produced many excellent pieces, failed financially one after the other, the last one in 1790.

BELGIUM

One of the most important factories of soft-paste porcelain was at Tournai. One of its services is famous, with a decoration of birds taken from the works of Buffon: it consists of 950 pieces. Tournai china is of fine quality and the colours are soft and delicate.

Plate, Buen Retiro , c. 1770 (right). — The porcelain of Buen Retiro near Madrid is somewhat rare as the factory was short-lived. The flower decoration indicates that the painters of Buen Retiro worked from Chinese patterns. The plate is bordered with a narrow gold line.

In the illustration below, the teapot is from Vezzi (c. 1730), the coffee-pot and the cup and saucer from Cozzi (c. 1770). The decorations of the latter factory recall those of Meissen, which served as models; the decorations of Vezzi are more Asiatic in feeling.

Yellow
Green
Blue
Red
Purple
Brown
Misc.
colour
shiny gold
matt gold

THE TECHNIQUE OF PAINTING ON PORCELAIN

MATERIALS AND PLACE OF WORK

ORGANISATION OF THE WORKROOM

Carry out your work in a well-lit room facing north; this will save you a lot of eye strain. Beware of direct sunlight, it can produce some nasty surprises. For instance, certain gold paints when they have been exposed to the rays of the sun can crack afterwards in the firing. In a badly-lit room or when working at night, use an angle lamp with a 75-watt bulb which will enable you to throw the light exactly where it is needed. Do not use a weaker bulb because it is not the minuteness of the work which tires the eyes, but the lack of light in which to carry it out.

A good kitchen table serves perfectly as a work-bench. An extension could be added to it, either fixed or movable, but on the same level as the top of the table. This device will prove most useful as a support for the forearm, particularly when painting fine lines. Allow room for several shelves on which to keep objects in process of decoration. A small chest of multiple drawers will enable you to store paints in colour groups.

PAINT BRUSHES

Choosing the paint brushes is very important, particularly with regard to the quality of the bristles; they should preferably be made of sable and should be both supple and springy. Good paint brushes are handmade and the bristles are carefully selected and matched.

Certain brushes for painting on china are fixed to a quill which must be fitted on to a wooden handle. We advise handles of light-weight wood, as one should not be conscious of the weight of the handle; the centre of gravity should lie in the last third of the paint brush. One can also sharpen the free ends of these handles in order to use them for removing particles of unwanted paint. Real quill mounts, however, are being more and more superceded by imitation ones made of plastic.

Winsor and Newton, Wealdstone, Harrow, Middlesex, England have a vast range of china painting brushes:

Series 12, Nos. 1 to 5: shading or 'modelling' brushes. (Page 34, A.)

Series 16, Nos. 00 to 2: lining brushes (equally suitable for gold). (B)

Series 29, Nos. 00 to 1: lining brushes, but more supple than those of Series 16 (suitable for cornflowers). (C)

Series 3A, Nos. 2 to 6, Series 33, Nos. 2 to 6: for modelling large flowers. (D)

Series 14A, 'large flat': a brush for spreading background colour. (G)

If ordering from England is a problem, ask for comparable brushes from an art supply store.

Specialist firms supply 'slant cut' liners (E), as well as specially shaped stippling brushes (F). Liners are always mounted on quill, or on plastic simulated quill.

The best results are obtained from a brush when it has been in use for a certain length of time. But

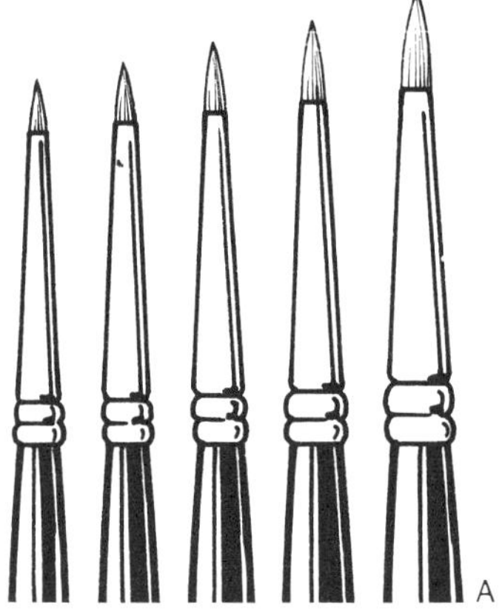

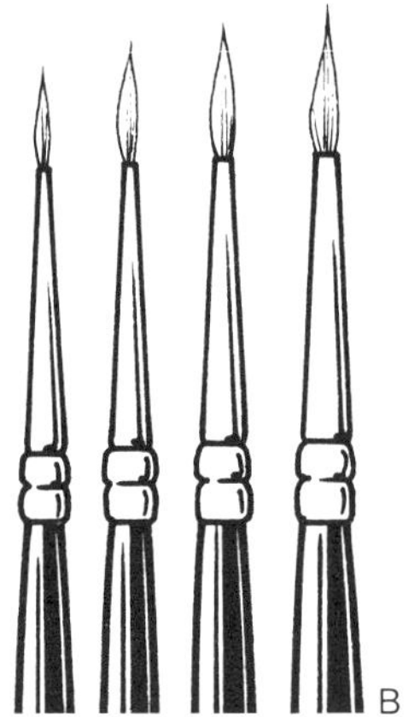

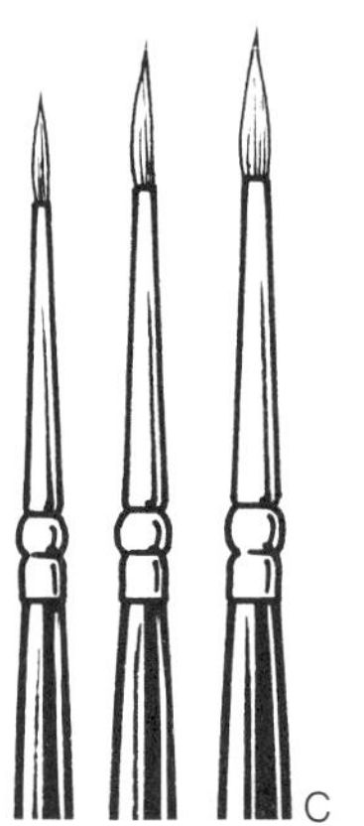

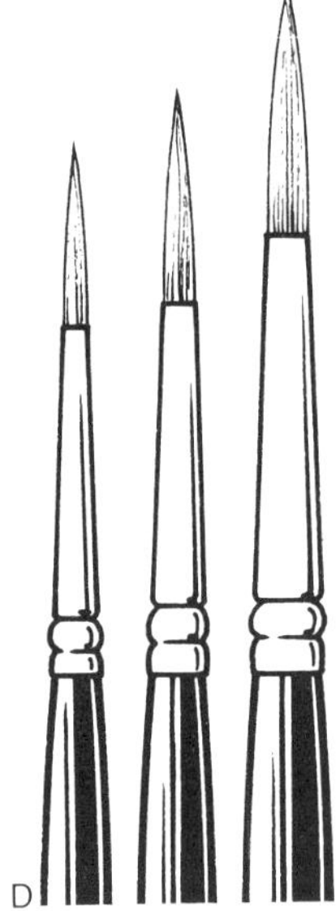

The forms and sizes of the paint brushes recommended are: A) shading or modelling brushes; B) lining brushes; C) fine lining brushes; D) large flower modelling brushes; E) slant-cut brushes; F) stippling brushes, and G) background-colour paint brushes.

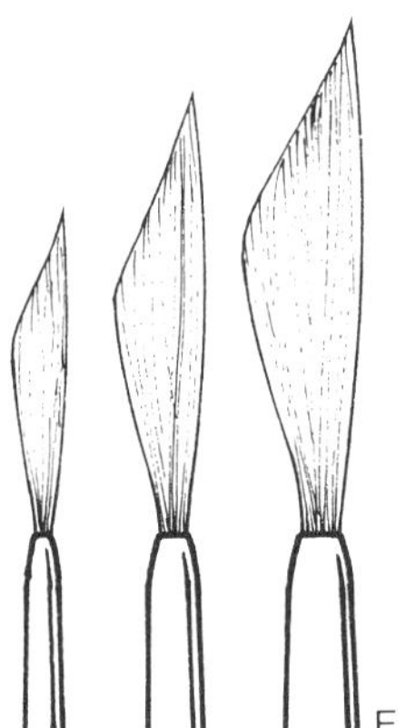

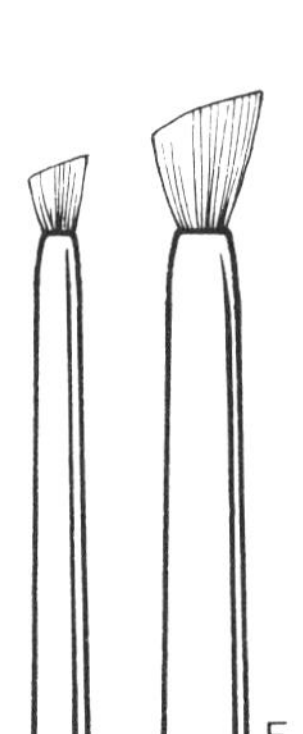

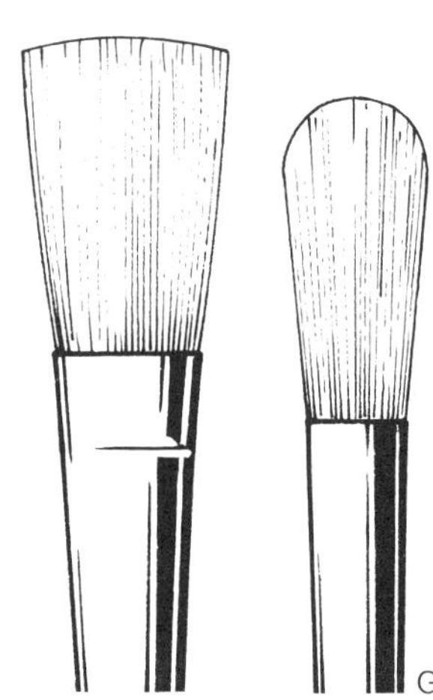

brushes which have been rubbed hard on a palette are soon spoiled, therefore they should be carefully dipped into the paint. After use, brushes must be thoroughly cleaned in spirit (methylated alcohol). They must then be soaked in turpentine or 'Medium' in order to preserve their shape and prevent the bristles from becoming too dry. If the brush is washed in spirit only, the dried bristles lose their suppleness and only regain their original shape with difficulty.

Brushes used for spreading background colour should be soaked in tepid soapy water until no trace of paint remains.

Brushes which have hardened can be softened by soaking them for a few minutes in spirit: they should never be put into too strong a solvent.

Each time a fresh colour is used, the brush should first be cleaned in turpentine or alcohol and afterwards wiped with a rag.

One should never use the same brush for gold as for paint. Gold is very sensitive and the slightest trace of paint can spoil its brilliance. Inversely, traces of gold in paint can introduce undesirable violet tones.

THE PALETTE KNIFE

A good quality palette knife is needed for mixing the paint. It should be made of stainless steel,

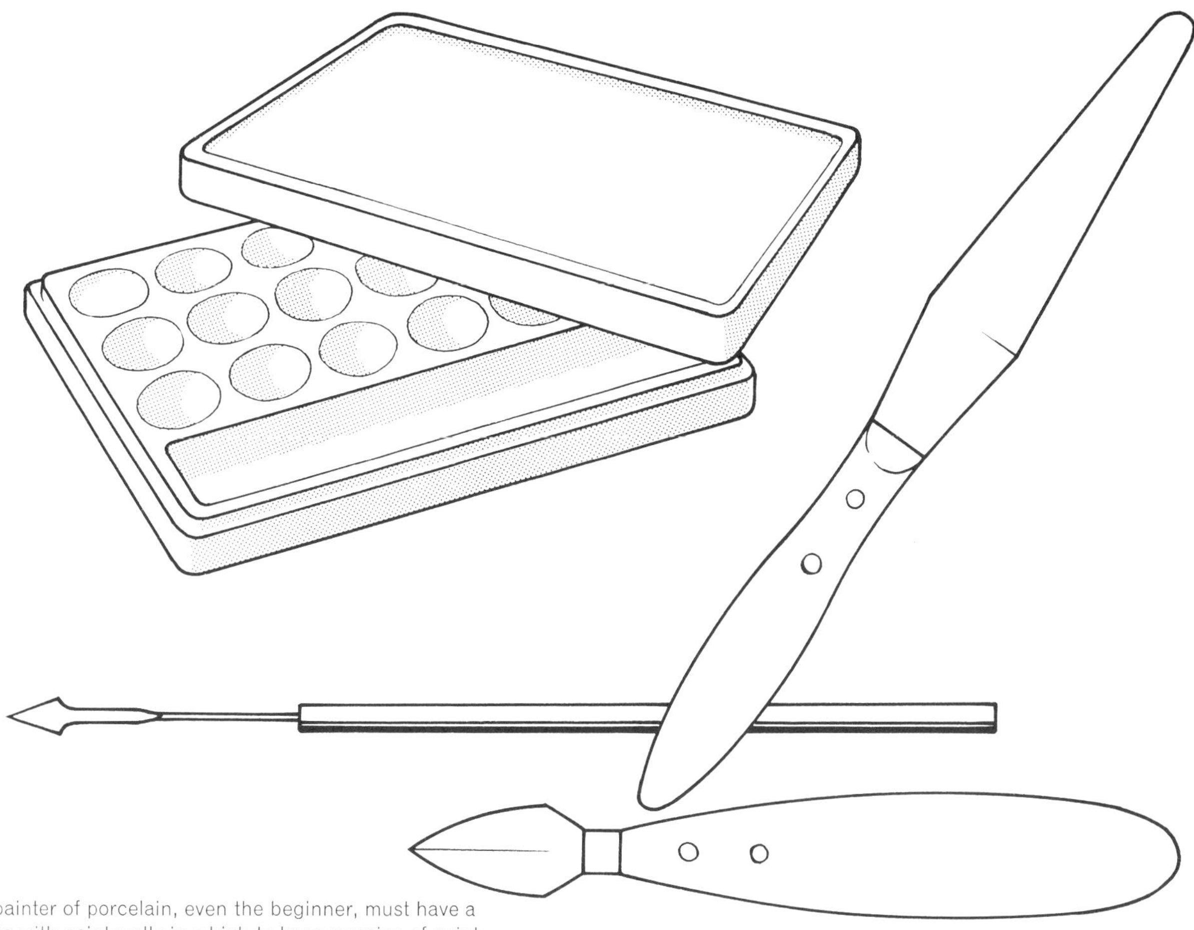

The painter of porcelain, even the beginner, must have a palette with paint wells in which to keep remains of paint (top), a stainless steel palette knife for preparing the paint (across), a scraper and a trimmer (bottom) for correcting small errors after the paint has dried.

neither too stiff nor too soft (the knife used in oil painting is definitely too soft and therefore not to be recommended). Here we must warn the reader against old-fashioned popular treatises in which the use of a horn or bone palette knife was recommended, rather than a metal one which, in those days, could have left traces in the paint and dirtied it. This argument was valid at a time when stainless steel was unknown. Moreover, horn or bone knives (the use of which we strongly deprecate) soon wear away when in contact with paint, leaving phosphates of lime in it. When the piece of china is fired, the lime acts as a solvent which can alter the fusibility as well as the tonality of the paint. The ideal length for the blade of the palette knife is 4 inches.

THE PALETTE, SCRAPER AND GLASS BOWL

A glass slab or a glazed tile of about 8×8 inches is recommended for use as a palette for preparing the paint. Always have two or three of these in reserve. Another palette with paint wells, provided with a lid, serves to keep remains of paint. A glass bowl with a lid will also be necessary for the exact amount of gold which you intend to use. A scraper or trimmer is a useful tool for correcting any mistakes due to clumsiness, after the paint has dried.

To burnish gold, either use burnishing sand kept in a small box specially for the purpose (left), or a 'scratch-brush', or spun glass burnisher (below).

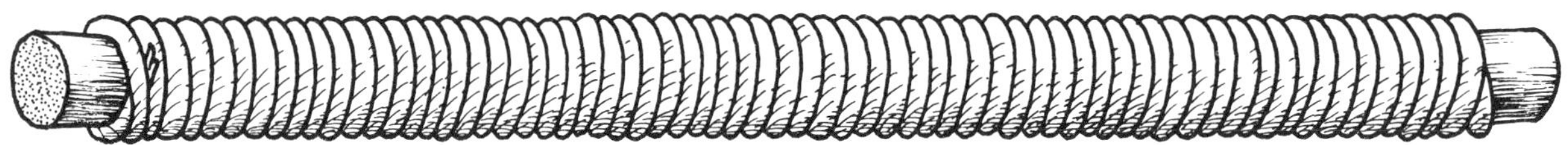

SPUN GLASS BURNISHER AND BURNISHING SAND

The spun glass burnisher is used for burnishing gold. Beware of short bristles which often get under the skin and cause painful irritation. Also, if after burnishing the gold any retouching is necessary, these small bristles should be very carefully removed as during the firing they would become embedded in the china and the piece would be irretrievably spoiled. Burnishing sand, if it is of good quality, can thus take the place of the spun glass burnisher, with advantage.

MISCELLANY

It is advisable to have several small glass or china receptacles handy, such as goblets, cups, egg-cups, liqueur glasses, etc. Metal and plastic materials should be ruled out because with metal there is the risk of oxides getting into the paint, and plastic can be dissolved by spirits and the paint thereby rendered useless. A clean linen rag will complete the equipment. Avoid using old material, even if it is clean, because the fragments of thread scattered over your workroom will inevitably end up in the paint: dust is Enemy No. 1 of the painter on china.

ESSENTIAL OILS, MEDIUMS, ETC.

Spirit (methylated alcohol): cleans brushes and all tools.

Thinner for Medium: dissolves paint which has already been mixed with 'Medium' and has dried and needs to be revived.

Turpentine and 'fat oil': extracts of pine resin. Turpentine mixed with 'fat oil' (which is no more than thick turpentine) is used to prepare paint according to the classical method. ('Fat oil' is available from suppliers of ceramic materials.)

Oil of cloves: extract of the immature flower of the clove (oleum caryophilli), is an essential oil, that is to say, it is soluble in spirit. It is used to stop paint from drying too fast when ground-colour is applied. Oils of lavender, carnation and rosemary have more or less the same properties.

'Médium Universel' (Schira, Lausanne): a product which conveniently replaces the classical mixture of oil and turpentine. Contains almost no turpentine, thus avoiding all allergies caused by this product; gives greater brilliance to the paint. Its main advantage, especially when too much has been used, is that it does not result in coagulation during firing.

Medium for use with gold: a solvent used to thin out gold when it has slightly thickened; should be added sparingly. The medium which is supplied by the manufacturer of the gold should be used.

Varnish: slightly gelatinous varnish which enables you to preserve white spaces when applying a

Left-overs of liquid gold can be carefully preserved in a bowl-shaped box with a lid, made of glass or china.

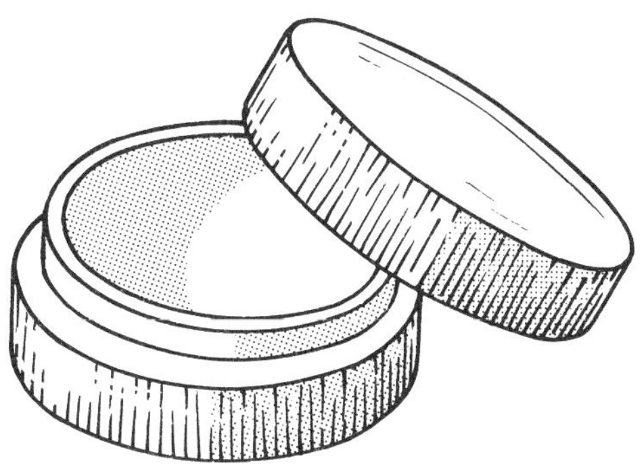

coloured background. Soluble in water, it is coloured red with fuchsine.

PAINTS

The paint used for decorating china is a special vitrifiable paint for use in the soft-firing process, that is to say, firing at a temperature of 1200 to 1500 degrees Fahrenheit: this should not be confused with under-glaze paint, which contains no vitrifiable matter. This special paint is made by first of all preparing a flux which is composed, in varying proportions, of white sand, minium and borax. This mixture is melted in a crucible and poured out as soon as fusion is complete. When it has cooled, it is mixed in the correct proportions with colouring matter and the whole thing is very finely pulverised. Colouring matter is obtained by dissolving metal oxides in hydrochloric acid and by precipitating them by means of carbonate of soda. The precipitate is then washed and carbonised till it is red-hot.

To put it more simply, ceramic paint is a kind of coloured and pulverised glass, and therefore translucent. It will be seen later why it is important to remember this peculiarity.

The only metals which can be used in their unaltered state for decoration are gold, platinum and silver. In fact they are the only ones which are resistant to heat and the process of oxidisation. In more primitive times, gold leaf and honey were ground up together and a flux added after washing the mixture. This onerous and meticulous procedure has been conveniently superseded by colloidal gold or platinum, which is made on the principle of dissolving the metal in aqua regia. The manufacturers of ceramic paints now produce liquid golds and platinums of excellent quality. Nevertheless, one should always insist on a matt gold assaying at least 30 % of metal. The economy effected by buying gold of a low percentage is not worthwhile, as much retouching will be necessary to hide the faults which will appear after firing.

To end the section on paints, we give a list of the colours obtainable from different metal oxides.

Iron: red, brown. A certain purple can also be obtained, according to how the flux is made up. Iron also comes into the making of certain blacks.

Copper: produces a beautiful turquoise blue when prepared with an alkaline flux, and produces a green of varying intensity when used with a lead-based or boracic flux.

Chrome: depending on the composition of the flux, produces yellows, yellowish-greens and bluish-greens.

Cobalt: a powerful colorant which gives an intense blue and, when mixed with other oxides, produces different shades of blue.

In this example of flower bunches in the Meissen manner, it will be seen that the details are carefully thought out and drawn with great delicacy. Large bunches are often accompanied by small ones: these are also scattered freely.

Manganese: sometimes combined with iron to obtain different shades of brown. Forms part of practically all the various blacks.

Antimony: mixed with iron and lead oxides, produces a fine range of yellows and oranges.

Gold: used in chlorinized form, provides a colour range from pink to purple and, when mixed with chlorinated tin, turns into a violet purple.

Silver: used in chlorinated form, produces a rather fresh yellow.
Paints for over-glaze decoration provide infinite possibilities. Firing at a low temperature allows the use of numerous metal oxides which furnish a rich colour palette. Certain manufacturers list a choice of several hundred shades. But the beginner should start with about six colours, and as his knowledge gradually widens, he should enlarge his palette with up to thirty shades; it would however be a mistake to reduce to anything less than this.

Basic colours

Cornflower-blue • moss-green • rosy-purple • rich purple • buttercup-yellow • copper-red

Colours for an enlarged palette

Yellow-green • olive-green • blackish-green • blue-green • buff-grey • sky-blue • gold-violet • brownish-yellow • reddish-brown • dark brown • chalk-white • blue-grey • cobalt blue • black

We advise beginners to use powder paints and to buy them in small quantities. There are also paints in tubes which are already mixed with fat oil and turpentine, but they are just as inconvenient to use as tubes of gouache.

Two methods of mixing paint

Successful painting depends largely on the mixing of the paint. The quantity prepared should be no more than the exact amount needed at the time.
Powder paint mixed with fat oil and turpentine (see Exercise No. 1, Cornflowers): First, stir the powder with the turpentine to produce a smooth paste. Add a few drops of fat oil. If the mixture is correct, the application of the paint should be easy. The paint should not spread when applied nor should it run unevenly from the brush.
Powder paint mixed with a special medium sold under the trade name 'Medium': stir the paint with several drops of 'Medium' until a smooth paste is obtained, then add 'Medium' drop by drop until the paint can be applied with ease. The product known as 'Medium' is better in several ways then the old-fashioned mixture of fat oil and turpentine: if too much 'Medium' is mixed with the paint it does no harm, at worst only lightening the colour. Here we would like to draw the reader's attention to an important fact. If when using the traditional method of mixing medium too much fat oil is used, two tiresome accidents can result, according to the shape of the painted surface: during firing the paint is liable either to run,

◁ By concentrating the decoration on the plate's rim, both very ornate and simple airy garlands can be used. These four examples represent typical patterns from the old porcelain factory at Nyon.

Right: The palette can be made on a large white flat plate, with or without a rim. Apply the colours with brushstrokes from the inside towards you. Write the number of the colour next to each sample and the manufacturer's name in the centre of the plate for accurate re-ordering of the paints.

or to coagulate. Colours based on gold, such as pinkish-purple, rich purple and violet need stirring far longer, or even mixing a day in advance. If this is done, the paint should be covered over with an upturned cup.

If the paint thickens while you are using it, add a drop of 'Medium' (or turpentine if you have already mixed the paint with oil and turpentine) and stir well. Care must be taken to see that the paint is of a good consistency, neither too oily nor too dry. It should go on easily.

PREPARATION OF A COLOUR PALETTE

In order to familiarise oneself with the various colours, the beginner is advised to prepare a colour palette. This is the most practical way of learning how the paints change colour during firing.

The procedure is as follows—

1. Make up a list of colours, beginning with the palest yellow, through the reds, browns, purples, violets, blues, grey-greens, and grey, to black.

2. Mix the paints to correspond with the list of colours.

3. Take a large flat plate, either with or without a rim, having first cleaned it with spirit.

4. Take up a little paint on the brush but never plunge the brush in up to the handle, the upper part of the bristles should be free of paint.

5. The paint is applied to the edge of the plate in a few straight brushstrokes, from the inside towards the outside (from the centre of the plate in the direction of the painter). Do not rub the brush about in the paint in different directions. The first brushstroke will produce strong colour, the ensuing ones becoming paler and paler; the last one should be quite transparent. By pressing the brush down with varying strength, different degrees of intensity of colour can be obtained in one stroke. The object is to produce a colour scale ranging from the deepest shade to the palest, in a space measuring ¾×1¾ inches. If the first brushstroke does not produce a deep enough colour, a second layer of paint must be applied. On the other hand, too thick a layer of paint has a tendency to crack and scale off. When the outside edge of the plate is filled with samples of paint, the process is continued on the inside. The number of the paint should be written above each sample thus shown; this is best done with a mapping-pen rather than with a brush, and the paint should be rather more liquid than for the brush. A few drops of oil of cloves can be added to maintain this fluidity.

It is not absolutely necessary to set up a colour palette before having begun the first exercise in painting. On the contrary, it is desirable to have already acquired a little practice in the art of mixing paint.

1st EXERCISE

Mixing the paint and the first brushstrokes

Bearing in mind that china paint is translucent, it is easy to understand that the superimposition of several layers of paint, or an accumulation of paint, will produce ever-greater depth of colour. There is thus no resemblance between painting on china and ordinary oil or gouache painting. Indeed, in the two latter techniques the thickness of the paint does not deepen the colour.

The function of the brush when used according to our method is therefore decisive, for it not only enables the paint to be applied, it also carries out the modelling and shading.

So let us begin our first lesson. It will be the most exacting one; but once it has been mastered, progress will be all the quicker.

Our teaching method is based on the modelling of the cornflower, which is so beautifully stylised by the painters of the Nyon factory. As a surface on which to practise, choose a plain-shaped plate of 7 ½ to 10 inches in diameter, and wipe it with a rag soaked in spirit. With your palette knife, take a quantity of cornflower blue paint equivalent in bulk to a small pea. On a glass slab, work a few drops of turpentine well into the powder.

A firm smooth paste without lumps should result, to which *one* drop of oil is added: stir quickly. Otherwise, instead of mixing the paint in this old-fashioned way, you can mix it by adding one or two drops of 'Medium' to as much paint as will go on the tip of the palette knife (see below). By means of a fine brush (of 'liner' quality, Series 29, No. 00), take a bead of paint the size of a pin-head on the tip of the brush. To do this, the brush should not be immersed in the paint, but the bead of paint should be lifted upwards by pushing the tip of the brush into the edge of the pool of paint with an upward movement. If you have arranged your workroom as recommended, with your left hand press the plate under the edge of the extending shelf of your table; this extension will also serve as a support for your right forearm. If you have a table only, without an extension, you can keep the plate still by propping it against the back of your left hand without too much strain. In this case, the only point of support for the right hand holding the brush will be the tip of the little finger resting against the table.

The first exercise consists of the shaping of exclamation marks; their longitudinal axis is the stroke formed by the brush. These are the petals of the cornflowers.

This exercise may seem over-simplified, but you will soon see that it poses several problems. First of all, diligence is required to make these petals all the same length (the ideal being ¼ inch), and to make sure that the shading is correct and the shape harmonious.

The brush should be dipped afresh into the paint for the modelling of each separate petal. If the

A plate is held on the wide-open palm of the left hand (left-hand sketch). When painting, the right side of the plate must be propped against the top of the table; it will thus be immobilised between your left hand and the table. With your right hand leaning against the edge of the table, you will be able to paint without your hand shaking (right-hand sketch).

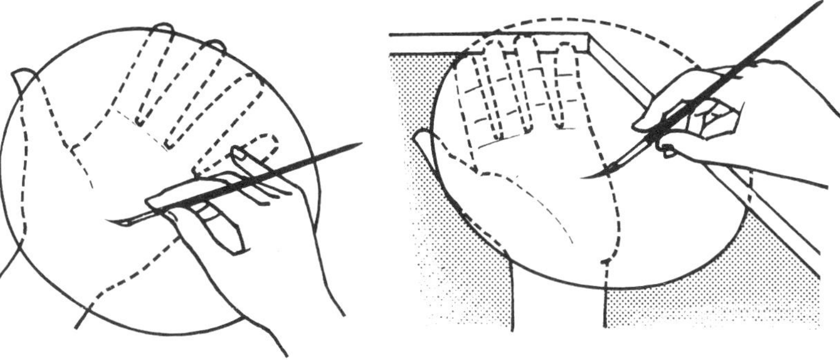

To paint a cornflower, a movement must be made with the brush as indicated in the sketch (right), and a small globule of paint lifted up, as in the second sketch (far right).

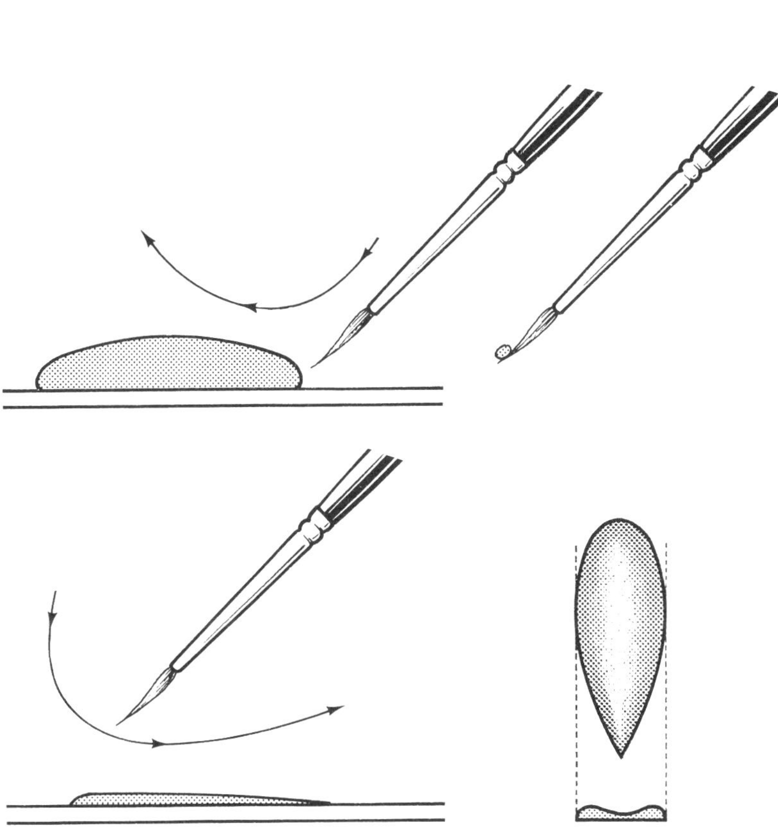

The diagrams show first, the movement of the brush when applying the paint to form a cornflower petal and secondly, the ground plan and section of the resulting petal as it should appear.

mixture is correctly proportioned, the paint should become matt a few minutes after application. If there is too much oil, the colour will spread and the modelling will disappear. In this case, more powder should be worked in, or better still, a new petal painted—this applies particularly to blue, which should always be freshly mixed. Let us now describe the brushstroke. With both hands supported as described above, a steady approach should be made towards the plate with the tip of the brush, loaded with its globule of paint. At the moment of contact light pressure should be applied to the brush, which will make the bristles spread out. The brush should then be drawn along the surface, the pressure becoming progressively lighter. The brush will barely touch the plate as it is withdrawn, thus ending the petal in a sharp point. This movement is effected by the action of the thumb and the index finger only, and once you have mastered it you will soon acquire the suppleness of fingers needed to carry out the following exercises with ease.

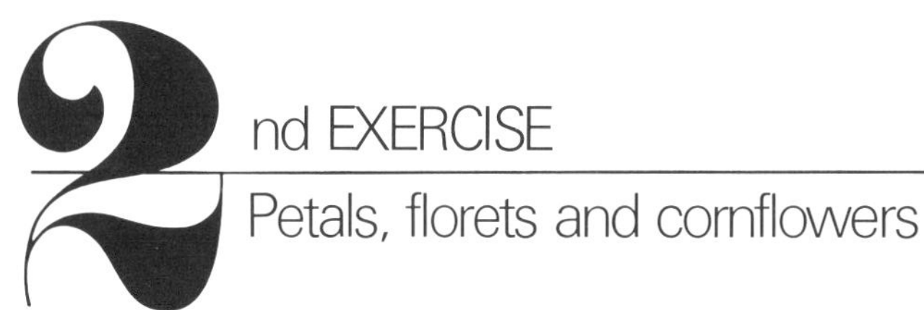

2nd EXERCISE
Petals, florets and cornflowers

Once you have achieved about fifty perfect exclamation marks you will be able to tackle the second phase of the exercise, that is the joining together of three of these petals to form a floret. The method is to add two lateral petals to the central one, of the kind you have just learned to make; these two laterals should be exactly the same shape as the central one, but shorter by a quarter (about 1/8 inch). Their longitudinal axes should converge at the base of the central petal. The outline of the central petal will only appear in its upper half. All that now remains is to dispose the florets thus formed in groups of two, three, four and five to complete the cornflower in its various aspects.

Note: avoid a cross shape when making a cornflower with 3 or 4 florets.

After a few hours of practising these shapes, you will acquire sufficient skill to start on your first pieces. We will now describe the different stages in detail, up to the point of firing: it will be a plate decorated with a scattering of cornflowers.

Having carefully cleaned the plate with spirit, mark the place for the centre of each flower with a cross or a dot. To draw on china, use an All Stabilo pencil which leaves no mark whatever after firing. Discard from your outfit all greasy pencils, or inks which will leave red (iron oxide) marks which remain after firing. Make the first dot 5/8 inch from the edge of the plate. Scatter the rest all over the surface of the plate, spacing them about 1 1/2 inches apart, while preserving a blank space of 5/8 inch all around the edge of the plate. Taking each dot as forming the centre of a cornflower, spread the flowers evenly, giving them one, two, three, four or five florets each. It is now that your aesthetic sense will come into play. Moreover, these flowers will have 'tails', or stalks; it is up to you to vary them by curling them in different directions, so that no two neighbouring cornflowers slant the same way or have the same number of florets. Another mistake to avoid: never place a flower in the geometric centre of the piece, thus providing it with an inartistic navel!

A small amount of green paint should now be mixed, preferably a soft yellow-green, the colour of young foliage. Allow the same proportion of medium as for blue.

Having mixed the paint, take the same numbered liner brush as for the cornflowers and first make a little dot at the point where the two, three or four florets meet, or right in the middle of the cornflower if it has five florets. From this point, draw a supple curving line of even thickness about ½ inch long. (To take care not to get two neighbouring cornflowers with parallel stalks, always paint the first stalk curving to the left and the next one to the right.) Still using the same paint and the same brush, paint the leaf: this is done with two strokes of the brush. At this point we can already put into practice the 'cornflower

The illustration below shows, in separate stages, the way to paint a cornflower (slightly enlarged here for clarity). In the top row are cornflower buds or florets; in the middle row, the opened cornflower with two, three, four and five florets. The bottom row shows how inartistic a cross-shaped cornflower can look and how, to the contrary, a five-petalled cornflower is a pleasing design.

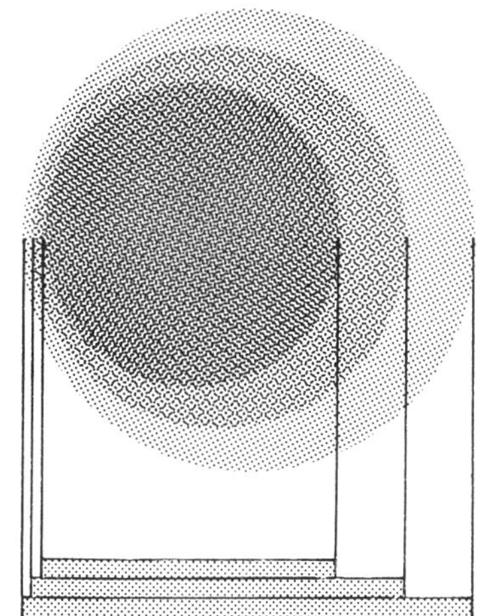

As ceramic paint is translucent, the superimposition of several layers of the same colour will give an increasing depth of tone. This diagram shows three superimposed layers of one colour and the different effects of density they produce.

technique': with a single dip into the paint, make two shapes like the cornflower petal, but curved and with the sharp point of the first one joining the stalk of the cornflower and melting into it. The second brushstroke will begin at the same point as the first one, that is to say, it will be superimposed on the first one at the departure point; it will then curve outwards, away from the stalk, in an opposing curve. As this green is not 'modelled' with the brush, the paint is taken up in a slightly different way to that recommended for the cornflower petals: the brush should be dipped into the edge of the pool of paint with a downward movement and drawn along so that the whole length of the bristles is covered in paint. With the brush thus filled with paint, one is able to paint the stalk and the leaf without needing to take more paint.

Whereas the axis of the brush was held at a perpendicular angle to the plate when painting the cornflower (which is rectilinear), it must be held at an oblique angle when painting the leaf. On the other hand, the stalk must be shown by a line of even thickness, and in order to paint this, the brush must be held at a completely vertical angle. Once the paint is thoroughly dry, the cornflowers must be completed by painting in their 'whiskers' and by shading the leaves. As both of these operations are carried out in the same colour, a rich purple, they are usually grouped together in the final phase and you must use the finest brush you possess. Mix the purple in the same way as the green, but slightly less liquid. Take up the paint by skimming over it and at the same time lightly rotating the brush between finger and thumb with a screwing movement. Between each floret of the cornflowers, insert a 'whisker', which is done by drawing an extremely fine and supple line coming out of the centre of the flower: each line should be scarcely longer than the floret itself. Still using very fine lines, shade the calyx on its right side and its underneath, the stalk on its right, and each part of the leaf on its upper edges. Cornflowers can be of various sizes according to the size of the piece you want to decorate: nevertheless, they should be the same size on all of the pieces of one service.

It may cause some surprise that we should take the cornflower as our point of departure. We must say straightaway that learning to paint a cornflower correctly, which is within everyone's reach, is the best way to acquire a good touch with the paint brush and the necessary suppleness of wrist to control the brush and not become its slave.

So here is your plate with its scattering of cornflowers completed, at least as regards the colours. There remains a very pretty trimming to be added to it: gold florets. They will fill up the spaces between the cornflowers.

When painting a scattering of cornflowers, any tiresome symmetry in the placing of the flowers must be avoided. The procedure should be as shown in the sketch. Cornflowers and gold florets are shown life-size, but a little closer together than we would recommend in actual practice.

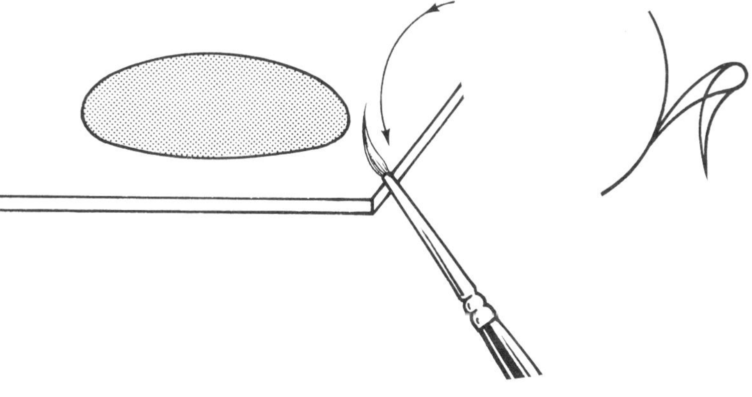

To paint the leaves of the cornflower, the brush should be used obliquely when taking up the paint, as shown on the right. Far right: outline of a leaf.

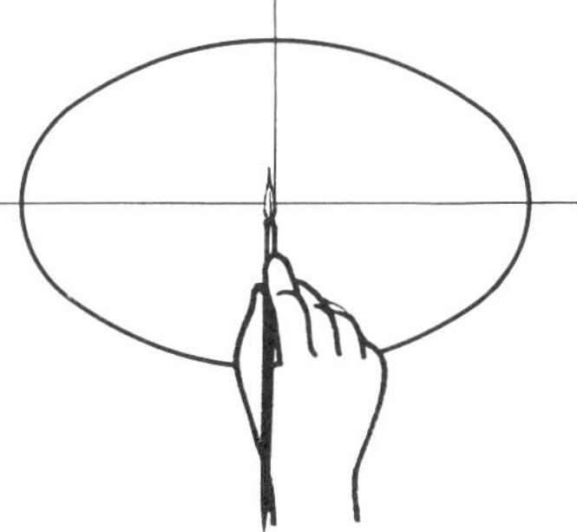

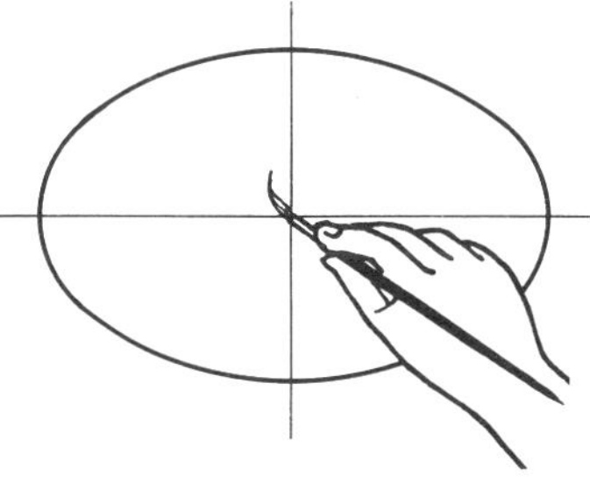

These diagrams show two very different ways of applying the paint. On the left, at a perpendicular angle when painting the cornflower petals: on the right, at an oblique angle when painting the leaf and the stalk of the cornflower.

3rd EXERCISE

Matt gold, gold florets, and borders

Let us here take the opportunity to give a definitive account of the preparation of matt gold. As the gold forms a deposit at the bottom of the bottle, it must be mixed before use. To obtain an evenly mixed substance the bottle must be shaken hard for several minutes. Some people advise the use of a small glass rod to stir up the gold but, in our opinion, this method does not produce good results and each time the glass rod is used an appreciable amount of gold is lost. Once the liquid is even, pour four or five drops into a small glass bowl, and it is ready to use. As liquid gold is usually sold ready to use, there is no need to add any solvent. If, when painting is finished, good care is taken to cover the dish with the lid, the gold will hardly thicken and when adding fresh gold to this left-over, a liquid of a good density is obtained. Solvent should only be added sparingly as there is the risk of reducing the percentage of gold, and if it looks thin or uneven after firing a great deal of retouching will be necessary, with consequent waste of time and costly material! The gold floret, about ½-inch long, is made with seven brushstrokes. The first brushstroke forms the uppermost petal and is made by exerting brief pressure, followed by drawing a fine, slightly curved line. This leading petal is flanked by two others whose narrow ends join the central stalk at a tangent. In its turn, the stalk is flanked by two petals on each side: these are more detached in shape, and the two uppermost ones are joined to the stalk on its outside curve.

Let us complete this work by decorating the edge of the plate with a very pretty design, the dog's-tooth pattern. It consists of small rounded tile shapes (or slightly elongated semi-circles) touching each other, painted in the same gold and with the same size brush as the florets, that is to say a fine brush, Series 16, No. 0 or 00. It can be made of squirrel hair (which is cheaper than sable), as it need not be particularly sensitive. These 'dog's-teeth' must be drawn very regularly to make their full decorative effect, and in order to achieve this regularity without too much difficulty, it is best to draw a thin line with the special All Stabilo pencil, about ⅛ inch from the edge of the plate. Let us here take the opportunity to describe a little trick which will prove helpful when drawing these fine lines. Grasp the pencil between finger and thumb very near its point and move the middle finger down to where the lead begins: by resting this finger on the edge of the plate, it will be easy to guide the lead accurately to the right place. There will now be no difficulty in juxtaposing the little tiles: if drawn within the penciled line, they will be easily kept to a regular size. Once this work is finished, it only remains for you to inscribe your signature on the back of the plate (preferably in the form of an original motif) and take it to the specialist for firing.

All brushes used for the application of gold must be rinsed after use in the bottle of medium provided with the gold. The gold deposited at the bottom of this bottle can be used again. Never let the brushes used for gold come in contact with any liquids other than gold or the medium used for gold.

After firing, take a piece of cotton wool which has been soaked in water and squeezed out: lightly dab it in polishing sand kept in a small box. Grains of sand will adhere to the cotton wool. Polish the surface of the fired gold with this using a rotary movement: the gold thereby acquires brilliance.

In these two bunches of flowers painted in the Meissen manner, the composition should be specially noted: a compact group of 2 or 3 large flowers accompanied by several smaller ones forms the body of the bunch. From here, a few light flowered branches radiate and on each side a large flower stands out, arranged asymmetrically. ▷

Birds painted in the Sèvres manner are often of an exotic nature, with an amusing touch of fantasy. The absence of a cartouche gives the feeling of an open landscape, seen beyond a foreground of leafy branches.

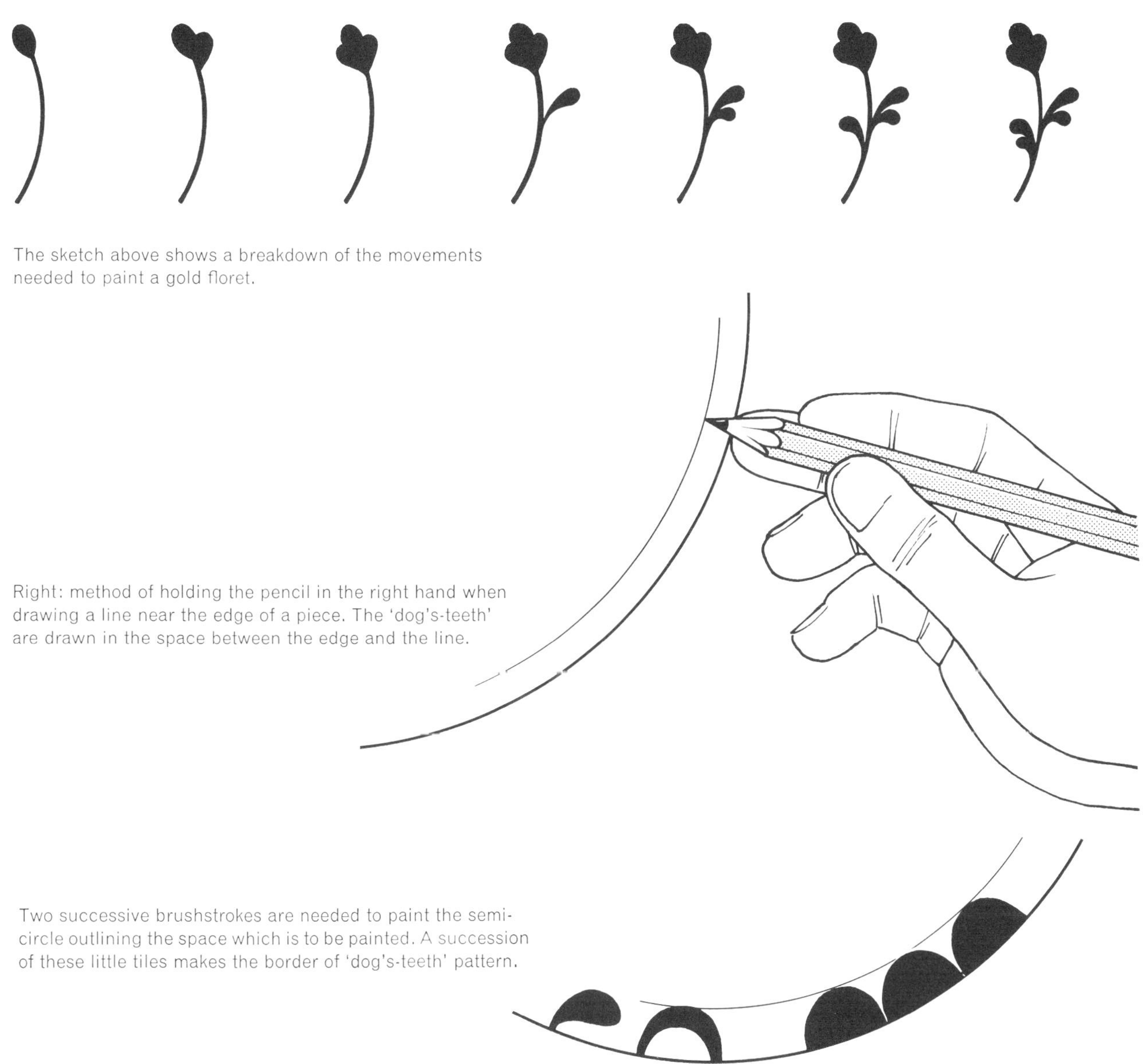

The sketch above shows a breakdown of the movements needed to paint a gold floret.

Right: method of holding the pencil in the right hand when drawing a line near the edge of a piece. The 'dog's-teeth' are drawn in the space between the edge and the line.

Two successive brushstrokes are needed to paint the semi-circle outlining the space which is to be painted. A succession of these little tiles makes the border of 'dog's-teeth' pattern.

4th EXERCISE

Roses and rosebuds

Designs with scattered mixed flowers usually include roses, rosebuds, daisies both full-blown, half-open and fading, forget-me-nots and their buds, and pimpernels. As with the scattered cornflowers, a space must be reserved for a gold floret between each little flower.

All of these flowers are stylised and painted with the minimum of brushstrokes. The stylishness of these brushstrokes gives the flower its character and freshness.

Let us begin by describing the making of a rose. Take up some paint on the fine brush (Series 12, No. 1) from the pool of already mixed purplish-pink paint by sliding the brush in sideways, so that there is paint along the full length of the bristles. Now visualize a circle about ¼ inch in diameter. The first brushstroke fills in the left edge of the circle but, by giving the brush some pressure to one side (quite hard at first and gradually diminishing), the paint is pushed towards the outside edge of the circle, thus lightening the colour towards the middle, which will give roundness to the rose. The second brushstroke is meant to define the heart of the rose, and outlines a little circle of about ⅛ inch diameter at the top of the ¼ inch circle, that is, at the point of departure of the brushstroke. The rose is now modelled, but it still has to be provided with two petals on either side. These are drawn in the same way as the cornflower petals, but in a harmonious curve following the outline of the rose. It is logical to begin with the upper petal, as the lower one will cover the lower half of the first one. Avoid leaving a white 'eye' in the middle of the rose, and do not let the petals look detached from the body of the flower. With the fine liner brush dipped in moss-green paint, draw a curved line of about ½ inch to represent the stalk of the rose. On each side of the stalk paint a sepal of the calyx. These are done in one brushstroke, with pressure exerted in the middle of the movement.

Having mixed a small quantity of rich purple, let us now proceed to the final touches. Two very fine curving lines at a tangent to the heart of the rose will give the outline of two petals which are still completely joined to the centre. With the same colour and in the same way as for the cornflower, paint some very fine lines to shade the outside edges of the stalk and the right side of the leaflets. The stylised thorns are indicated by three slightly fan-shaped lines painted across the stalk almost perpendicularly.

Let us now discuss the rosebud. With the fine modelling brush dipped in purplish-pink, a kind of inverted V is made, but with one side slightly longer than the other. The petals of a rosebud beginning to open are thus suggested in two brushstrokes. Taking the liner brush dipped in moss-green, the sepals surrounding the petals are now painted in, with a long supple S-stroke thickening towards the tip. The right sepal is painted first, curving upwards at the bottom of the S, to finish between the two branches of the inverted V; the left one, which begins a little lower than the first, finishes at the base of the bud. As with the cornflower, make a dot for the calyx and a thin curving line of about ¼ inch for the stalk. There are no leaves or thorns to encumber this delicate flower. As with the foliage of the cornflower and the rose, the shading is done with rich purple on the right side of the leaflets, calyx and stalk.

This illustration is devoted to the rose. The top row shows the progressive development of the corolla. The middle row indicates how to complete the flower and give it an appearance of lightness and shapeliness. The bottom row gives in detail the successive stages in the formation of a rosebud.

5th EXERCISE
Daisies, forget-me-nots and pimpernels

The daisy is spread among the scattered flower patterns in three different shapes: half-opened, full-blown and wilting; all three forms are stylised as usual. The colour used is sometimes cornflower-blue, sometimes copper-red.
The half-opened daisy consists of three petals like the cornflower but, unlike it, these petals are separate, although converging at the same point. Again, the calyx is made with a dot and the stalk with a curved line. The leaf, again flanking the exterior of the curve, is made with three brush-strokes as with the cornflower leaf, but this time the shape harmonises with the flower's curve. As with the flowers we have already studied, the stalk and the leaf are shaded on the right side with rich purple paint.
The full-blown daisy is a little masterpiece of stylisation. It is drawn within an imaginary circle of about ¼-inch diameter. As this flower is shown in half-profile, the length of the petals diminishes progressively towards the top, the last one being shown as a mere dot. Begin at the bottom with a completely vertical rectilinear petal, using the same brushstroke as for the first petals of the corn-flower and, *without taking any more paint on the brush*, form the right-hand lateral petals, curving them slightly and progressively diminishing their length until you reach the uppermost petal, which will be a dot. Dip again into the paint and repeat the process on the left-hand side. Care must be taken to leave a white space at the base of the petals. This space, in the shape of a horizontal oval, will be filled with a blob of buttercup-yellow to represent the receptacle or torus of the flower. As the daisy has so many petals it would look unbalanced if it were supported by one stalk only as in the case of the rose; it has therefore been given a double stalk to which the leaves (shaped like those of the budding daisy) are attached in a less stiff way. The shading is done in the way previously described for other foliage. The recep-tacle, the oval yellow blob in the middle of the flower, is shaded by a dot at its centre and a curve at its base, still in the same rich purple.
The wilting daisy differs from the full-blown one only in the number of petals and the shape of the second stalk. In fact, after forming the first recti-linear petal and the lateral petals on one side of it, do not paint any lateral petals on the other side. The yellow receptacle is of course left intact. The picture thus formed is of a daisy which has lost half its petals. The first stalk is still the same as before, that is to say, a simple curve; as for the second, this now curves gracefully all round the petals, completing this picture of a fading flower with a weak tired stalk.
The forget-me-not is represented in half-profile, like the full-blown daisy. Nevertheless, its rounded petals are painted in five oval blobs of different sizes. These five petals are painted in cornflower

This sketch shows the little flowers which make up the multi-flowered pattern of the plate on page 83. The first five drawings in the top row indicate the movements used in painting the full-blown daisy, and the two last ones those for the wilting daisy. The second row shows how to draw the budding daisy, and the last three drawings in this row define the movements used for the pimpernel. Instructions for the forget-me-not and its buds are in the bottom row.

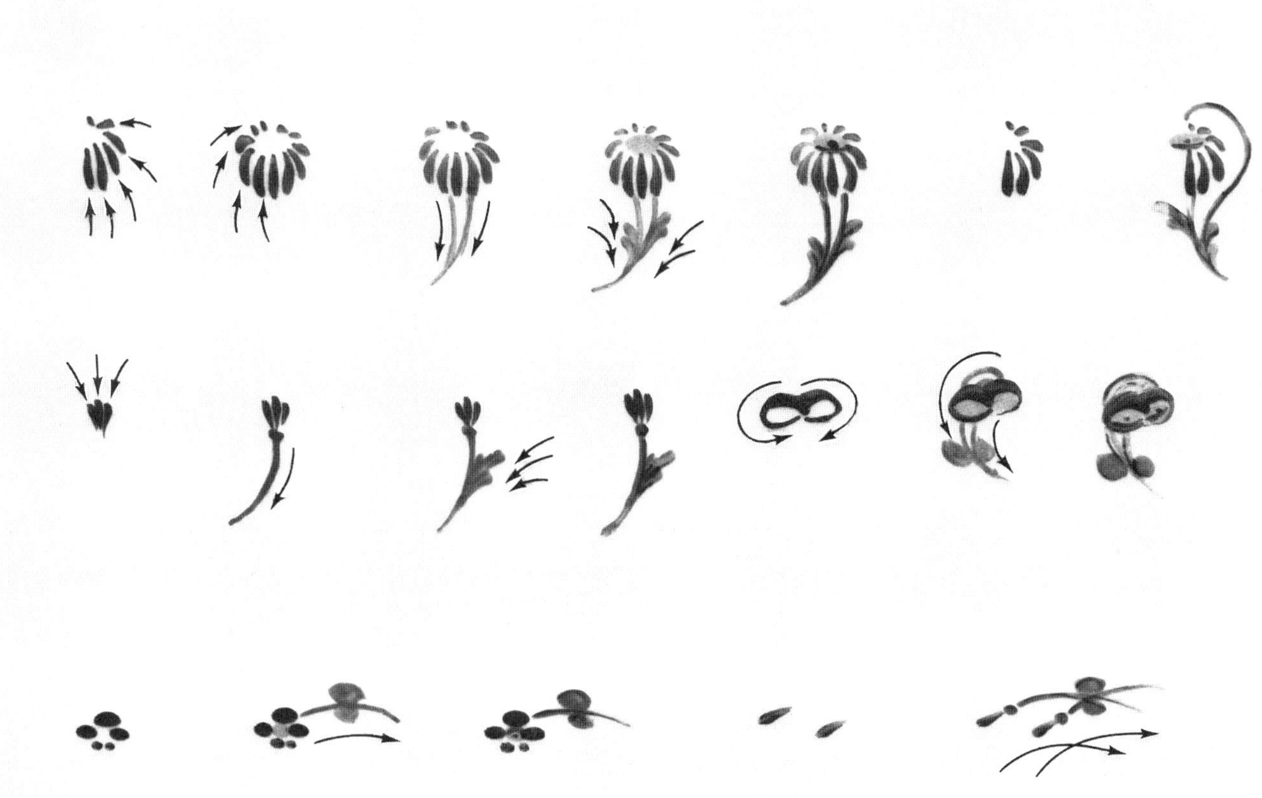

Flowers painted in the Sèvres manner, although always stylised, have a strongly naturalistic look. The cartouches framing these bunches add a romantic note and show them off advantageously. These cartouches are painted gold, shaded with brown, either with or without a previously applied relief pattern to take the gold. ▷

blue or copper-red, with a single dip into the paint. The largest petal is painted first, followed by one medium-sized one on either side. There will be enough paint left on the brush to paint the two smallest ovals, the colour by now being paler. These five petals cluster round another oval, the yellow receptacle. The stalk is still formed by a gracefully curved line; two round leaves are added to it, a small one inside the curve and a larger one outside it.

As the forget-me-not bud is very slender, there are always two of them, on two overlapping curved stalks each ending in a calyx and a petal and with a small round leaf on the inside of the curve and a larger one on the outside.

The pimpernel is painted either in cornflower-blue or copper-red, exactly like the forget-me-not and the daisy. With a single dip into the paint, make two ovals: the top edge of the oval must be thickened by exerting slight pressure on the brush. The first oval, drawn with an anti-clockwise movement, must be a complete oval; but the second one, which goes clockwise, must be an incomplete oval. The central space in these two ovals is filled with yellow and shaded in the same way as the receptacle of the daisy. The double crook-shaped stalk is provided with two oval leaves of different sizes.

After sufficient practice in painting all these flowers, all that remains is to place them carefully on the object according to the same principle as that laid down for the scattered cornflowers pattern, by alternating the axes of the flowers, the curves of the stalks, and also the colours—for instance, placing a cornflower-blue one next to a copper-red one. Sufficient space must always be allowed between each flower for a gold floret. Finish the edge of the plate either with the 'dog's-tooth' pattern or with a thin gold line. Page 83 shows a plate decorated with the scattered multi-flower pattern.

You have now learned how to paint the multi-flowered pattern in which the rose and the rose-bud play a part. There is also another scattered pattern which is now within your reach: one which consists entirely of roses and rosebuds, as usual accompanied by gold florets.

What you have learned up to now is very important, because if you have acquired a certain skill in the making of these small flowers, a multitude of other patterns is now within your capability. All you need do is to transpose these flowers as, for instance, in a continuous garland round the rim of a plate or in looped garlands round the periphery. For this kind of pattern, care must be taken to divide the surface to be painted into equal parts: when forming the loop of the garland, the size and importance of the flowers must progressively diminish from the centre of the loop towards the two ends. Roses and rosebuds are very suited to this kind of pattern and also to the making of monograms.

6th EXERCISE

The small bunch

Before tackling the kind of flower composition which the Meissen and Sèvres factories produced in such masterly fashion, let us begin more modestly with the small bunch in the 'Old Paris' style. As this style represents the intermediary designs between the scattered multi-flower pattern and the large bouquet, it paves the way to the mastery of the more important compositions without too much difficulty. For the first phase, we suggest the informal flowery branches which are found in Nyon and Old Paris decorations. The size of the flowers on these branches is easily double that of the scattered flowers we have been studying. They look quite different because they have a less stylised appearance and are closer to nature without, however, a realism from which fantasy and individualism are precluded.

Let us begin with the rose. Having mixed a small quantity of pinkish-purple paint and the same amount of rich purple, immerse the full length of the bristles of a medium-sized modelling brush in two superimposed layers of paint; first the pinkish-purple and then the rich purple. In this way, you dip into two colours for the same brushstroke. The rose should be shaped as previously in the scattered pattern, but the size should be doubled. By pressing the brush down and spreading the paint either to right or left, subtle and beautifully effective variations of colour can be obtained with a single brushstroke. By varying the angle of the brush, this technique allows a petal to be given relief without superfluous retouching. A branch is drawn with one or two roses and a few buds on it; the leaves are more numerous, and as they are painted with the same technique using two colours on the brush at the same time, it is easy to model them attractively. We advise a yellow-green and an olive-green for the foliage.

Let us here mention parenthetically that it is essential to paint in an organic direction, that means, in the way in which the subject grows, whether it be the veins of a leaf or the hairs of an animal's fur. The tulip leaf with its rectilinear veins is painted in the direction of its length, whereas the rose leaf with its pinnate veins is painted with a succession of brushstrokes radiating widthwise from the central vein and ending at the outside edges. When the brush has been dipped in the two above-mentioned greens, a start is made at the base of the leaf, and without taking more paint the tip of the leaf is reached in successive waves of colour. The lateral veins will thus have been defined by progressively diminishing the depth of colour. The same procedure applies to the other half of the leaf. It will now have a rounded, attractively shaded appearance. This same technique can now be successfully used to paint sprays of forget-me-nots and marguerites. These sprays, either scattered or used as borders and garlands, are painted with a minimum of trouble and have great decorative value.

◁ As in the preceding illustration, the cartouche surrounding this bird decoration forms a complete frame. A cartouche is especially recommended where decoration has been applied to a reserved white area on a coloured background.

7th EXERCISE
The large bouquet

This subject deserves a whole essay to itself if a thorough study of each different flower in every style of painting is contemplated. But we must confine ourselves to a few words of advice, because our previous instructions should enable the amateur to give an intelligent rendering of any flower he may choose.

Above all, in order to give 'volume' to a bouquet, one must remember that it is not composed of flowers that have been pressed between the pages of a herbal, but of really fresh flowers artistically arranged. The second important point: it must be remembered that as the light comes from the upper left, the lower right-hand part of each flower or leaf will be the darkest. Similarly, according to the angle of the axis of each flower, a zone of light will be reserved when the colour is applied, and the shadow of the petals will be shaped in relation to the shape of the flower itself and its position in the bouquet.

The composition of the bouquet need not be bound by strict or precise rules and each painter can let his fancy run free by building up a bunch of wild flowers, flowering branches such as apple or lilac, or garden flowers such as roses, tulips and zinnias. One can also get excellent ideas by studying the flower paintings of the old Dutch masters and the pattern books sold in the trade.

Before embarking on the composition of a large bouquet it is as well to know the particular technique required in painting a few of the principal flowers such as the rose, tulip, poppy, marguerite etc., as well as the appropriate foliage.

Let us remember that the painter on china does not aim at a faithful copy of nature but at an evocation, which is in fact a representation of each flower with the minimum of detail.

For a start we will therefore apply ourselves to portraying each of these flowers in the simplest possible way. After having assimilated this technique, it will be a simple matter to add more detail by retouching, thereby approaching the techniques of Sèvres or Meissen.

MODELLING THE ROSE

1. Visualise a circle of about a $^5/_8$ inch diameter. With a long fine brush (No. 4) cover this surface with a film of rosy-purple paint (see page 62).

2. Next, take small amounts of rosy-purple and rich purple: then, with an upward movement of the brush, form the right petal with one brush-stroke; this petal is meant to be in shadow, since the light comes from above on the left. When removed briskly from the china, the brush will leave a slight ring which will indicate the rolled edge of the petal.

3. Proceed in the same way with the left petal, but without any paint on the brush, which is impregnated with 'Medium' only. This will have the effect of partially removing the ground colour formerly applied and of making (with the same abrupt removal of the brush) a rolled edge to this petal too, which is now in the full light.

4. With a brush lightly dipped in pinkish-purple, start modelling the middle petal from its base upwards: this is done with two strokes of the

brush, one on the right and one on the left. In so doing, the two petals first painted will be overlapped. The same withdrawal movement of the brush as before is used to mark the edge of the petal.

5. The shadows in the heart of the rose are suggested by one or two dark accents made with a brushful of combined rosy-purple and rich purple applied to the top left part of the small circle hitherto left untouched.

6. With two brushstrokes a petal is shown half attached to the left side of the rose. First mark the inside of this petal in a graceful curve with pinkish-purple on the brush; then wipe the brush and with an upward movement shape the outside edge of the petal.

7. With one brushstroke, make a supple curve in rich purple on the right side of the rose, thus forming the reverse of a petal.

8. Holding the brush almost horizontally, press it towards the base of the rose and then remove it sharply. This forms the rolled edge of a petal clinging to the right side of the rose. Depending on the length of the brush used, either one, two, or three strokes are needed.

9. Proceed in the same way with the lower left petal, but with very pale pinkish-purple, not forgetting that the light comes from the left.

10. Complete the rose with two lightly sketched petals, one on the right in rich purple, the other on the left in pinkish-purple.

The leaves which accompany this kind of rose must be modelled in a special way: once more using the long No. 4 brush, fill it with moss-green and blackish-green paint and using a spiral movement, paint the two halves of the leaf, starting from the central rib. Each half is painted in one stroke, without taking up extra paint. By following this method, the transverse veins will take shape automatically.

With the aid of a little imagination, it is easy to show some leaves in half-profile or with the underside showing. Some variation in the colouring of the foliage can be obtained by using combinations of other greens mixed with browns and purples. The same thing applies to the rose, which can be painted in grey and pink, yellow and red, or other colour combinations.

MODELLING THE TULIP

Let us begin by visualising an oval of about 1 ¼ inches long, which represents the most important petal seen in half-profile. From behind this petal and on each side of it parts of other petals emerge, which are the starting-point of the work of modelling. Use the same brush as for the rose, No. 4. The colours are buttercup-yellow and a pure red.

1. With wide brushstrokes of yellow combined with a little red, model the two petals emerging from behind the tulip. With a little more red than yellow, give them a reverse side (see page 62).

2. The most important stage is the modelling of the tulip's main petal. Its two halves are built up by brushstrokes which form graceful curves, starting at the top of the petal. First comes the

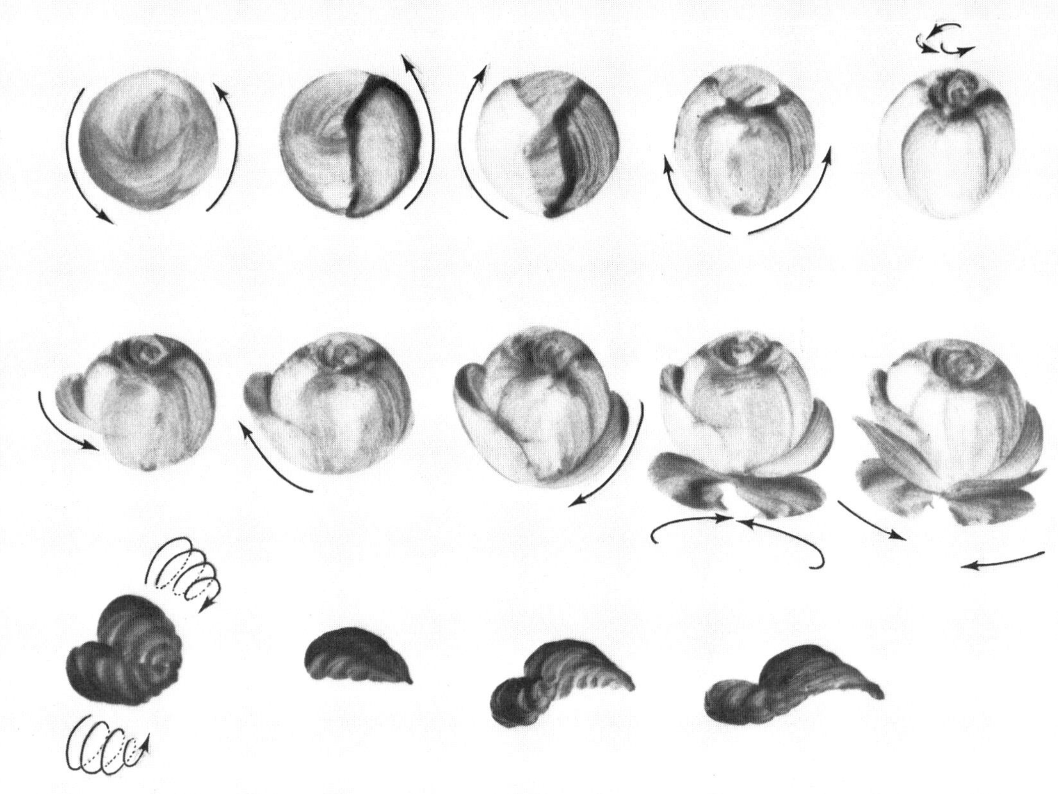

Opposite, above: the different stages in the modelling of the rose in a large bouquet. Top row: modelling the corolla. Second row: adding the slightly loosened lateral petals. Third row: modelling the rose leaf.

The tulip adds great charm to a large bouquet. The lower illustration opposite shows how to paint this flower. First row: first to be painted are the two petals which appear behind the main petal in the foreground, which will be painted in two stages. Second row: a petal seen in profile is half attached to each side of the flower. At the right side of the illustration is a tulip leaf.

left half, then the right half, both overlapping the back petals which were painted first. The convex curve of the petal and its central rib will thus be formed at the same time. To give it a certain importance in the bouquet several drooping petals may be added, giving it the look of an overblown tulip.

3. The drooping petal on the left: begin by painting the reverse of the petal in one brushstroke, with more red than yellow. Then, with the brush dipped in yellow only, vigorously fill in the rest of the petal, overlapping the preceding one.

4. The drooping petal on the right can be made with two or three brushstrokes, in yellow over-painted in red.

For the tulip leaf with its longitudinal veins, use the tip of the fine brush, which is held vertically. Using the tip of the brush only, exert alternate fairly strong pressure and relaxed pressure to obtain bands of varying colour. This first stage is done with moss-green; a few accents of olive-green give more movement to the leaf, which should have the wavy look which is typical of the leaf of the tulip.

MODELLING THE POPPY AND THE ANEMONE

The common characteristic of these two flowers is that they both have a corolla formed of large delicate petals. It is preferable to paint them in half-profile.

To do this, think of a cup or bowl in half-profile tilted towards the right. As the light comes from above on the left, it is easy to place the patches of light and shade on the flowers.

Depending on the size of the proposed flower, either a long No. 4 or No. 6 brush is used. The colours are a pure red for the poppy and grey, blue and black for the anemone.

1. Begin by painting the petals showing in the inside of the flower, two for the poppy and three for the anemone. With very diluted paint, take the right petal first. With a deeper shade, model the central petal and then, with a very deep shade, the left petal. These three brushstrokes are made from top to bottom, using almost the full length of the bristles (see page 65).

2. Model the two outside petals, beginning with the one on the right in very strong colour; the one on the left needs very weak colour. These two petals are worked from bottom to top, starting with the tip of the brush and gradually flattening it. Again, lift up the brush abruptly to form a small rolled edge at the top of the petals.

3. With a brushful of very diluted paint, the petal to the left of the flower is made by using the tip of the brush and gradually flattening it; as before, lift up the brush abruptly to make the rolled edge. Two brushstrokes of strong colour suggest two shaded petals to the right of the flower.

4. It now remains to fill the heart of this flower with a dome-shaped receptacle: this is carried out in diluted black and, once the paint is dry, it is decorated with black stamens.

The leaf which accompanies the poppy or the anemone is very decorative and adds a delightful

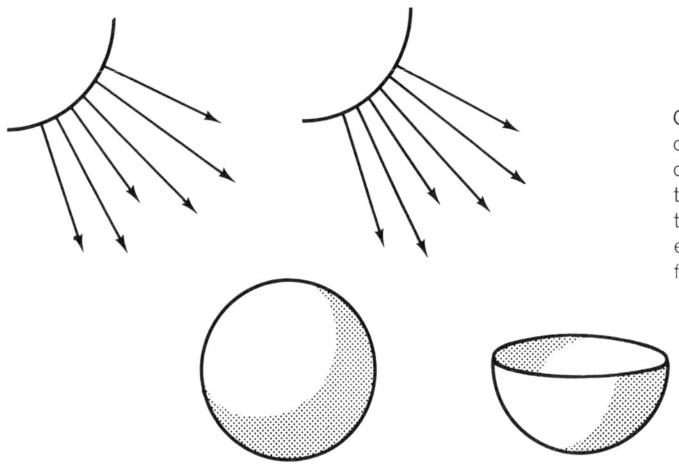

Opposite: The marguerite is painted in two stages. First, a row ▷ of dark petals which will appear below the upper half-circle of lighter coloured petals. Complete the flower by painting the receptacle, stalk and leaves. The second row shows how to paint the corolla of an anemone; first, the interior, then the exterior. The third row shows how to complete the flower by flanking it with two loose petals, and two others seen in profile.

Left: According to generally accepted principles, light strikes an object as shown in these diagrams. On the left: how to shade a convex surface and on the right, a concave one.

touch to a bouquet. It must have a graceful outline, and a greyer or bluer green must be used, by mixing yellowish-green with either grey-buff or myrtle-green. To give some life to this foliage, the undersides of the leaves must be modelled in darker colours such as olive-green or blackish-green.

MODELLING THE MARGUERITE

This flower can be painted in several colours, according to the composition of the bouquet; if a dark accent is desired, it can be violet or rich purple; for a medium tone, sky-blue or cornflower-blue; for a subtle effect, flat white with a hint of moss-green. By using permanent white for the last-mentioned combination, a light relief can be obtained as this paint produces a thicker coat than others: but care must be taken not to overdo this, as any paint which is put on too thick is liable to scale off after firing.

According to whether a full-face or a side-view marguerite is required, either a circular space or a very narrow oval should be reserved for the receptacle. Let us choose the intermediary shape.

1. With a large short-haired modelling brush (No. 3 or 4), begin by painting the lowest petals in a dark shade: these will hardly show in the finished flower.

2. Taking care to leave a small reserved area for the receptacle, paint the whole fringe of upper petals in a lighter shade, making them boldly overlap the petals first painted. In this way there will be no gaps.

3. The slightly domed receptacle is now painted yellow and shaded with little dots of chestnut-brown. In studying these few flowers and leaves we have touched on the technique of the different brushstrokes. With a little imagination and plenty of practice it will be easy enough to apply this technique to the painting of all sorts of flowers, from sweet peas to the most complicated orchids. As long as the organic form is respected, the desired effect will be achieved.

As for the composition of the bouquet itself, the surface area and the shape of the object to be decorated must be carefully considered. Then again, to make a balanced bouquet it is advisable to group two or three important flowers such as a rose, a large marguerite, an anemone, and surround them with some leaves which are close together and superimposed. A tulip and its leaves or a poppy with leaves and buds can be painted spreading outwards from this homogenous group. The base of this bouquet is supported by a group of small flowers such as colts-foot, immortelles or pimpernels. Introduce an airy look by adding a few grassy sprays painted in pastel colours such as grey, yellow, or very pale green. When the bouquet is finished, if there still seems to be too large an area of virgin china and it is impossible to add a flower without spoiling the balance of the bouquet, the addition of a butterfly or some other insect can solve the problem in an elegant manner.

8th EXERCISE

The application of background colour

It must be remembered that paint for china is composed of vitrifiable matter and pigment. When this paint is washed on as a fairly fine uniform background, the amount of vitrifiable matter is usually insufficient. It is therefore necessary to add a flux to it, in the maximum proportion of one third of flux (sold under this name commercially) to two thirds of paint. Too high a proportion of flux could considerably alter the strength of the colour. We strongly advise the use of 'Medium' as a binding agent, as it does not attract dust, unlike oil and turpentine medium. A few drops of spirits of cloves will prevent the mixture from drying too quickly. It is advisable to stir the amount of paint you are going to use for quite a long time and even to let it lie in a firmly closed receptacle for several hours before use. When applying a very pale background, increase the proportion of 'Medium'.

As previously recommended, the object to be decorated must be conscientiously cleaned with a good quality rag soaked in spirit. A flat 'fish-tail' shaped brush must be used, and not one which sheds its hairs; it must be big enough (Series 14 A large flat) to colour-wash the object as rapidly and smoothly as possible. Take a nylon–foam sponge and first secure it with an elastic band to avoid working with rough edges which would make marks on the background: spread the paint evenly in short light dabs. Put the object to dry somewhere dust-free. Drying can be speeded up by placing it under an infra-red lamp. Wait till the piece is completely dry before proceeding to clean the parts which are not going to be coloured, such as the interior, the lips and the handle of a cup. The foot of the object must also be carefully cleaned, as it could stick to its support during firing: this might cause small chips or lumps which would have to be rubbed down after firing. It is much more delicate work to apply backgrounds in dark colours such as black, Empire green or purple. Therefore we advise two applications, with one firing between them. The paint has to be more consistent and must be spread very minutely with the flat brush. As the layer of paint is automatically thicker with a dark background, we recommend first working over it with the stippling brush made of skunk-hair. The size of this brush varies according to the extent of the surface to be treated and the work is carried out in rapid, vigorous strokes. The effect of this is to disperse any agglomerations of paint which might cause scaling during firing. Indeed, these agglomerations would only be slightly leveled when using the foam sponge alone; this is used for smoothing the surface after the paint has been evenly dispersed with the stippling brush.

Depending on the result obtained after the first firing, a second coat of paint is applied, the thickness of the paint varying according to the required depth of colour. This second application is carried out in the same way as the first one.

If a hair from the brush or a particle of dust sticks to the piece, it must immediately be removed with a needle and the place smoothed over again with the sponge.

The illustration on the right shows five small terraced landscapes ▷ from the old Nyon factory: they are painted in the Marseilles style.

9th EXERCISE
The reserved areas on backgrounds

EXERCISE 10
Landscapes and birds

Beautiful effects are obtained by reserving unpainted areas on coloured backgrounds: they may either take the shape of a medallion which is afterwards filled with a flower or landscape decoration, or the outline of a bouquet, or any other theme of the painter's imagination.

A new and wonderful product exists to facilitate this work, called preserving varnish. This varnish, which is usually red, is used for covering the areas which are to be reserved, before painting in a colour background. It is applied in one rather thick coat with an ordinary quality brush. Let it dry thoroughly and then apply the background as previously described. Next comes a very delicate part of the operation: before the paint dries, take a very sharp pair of tweezers or a needle point, and very gingerly remove the film formed by the varnish. This operation has to be carried out with extreme care, and the varnish must be thick enough not to tear but to be easily removed from the china. In this way you will be able to reserve clean-cut medallions or cartouches or to pick out the outline of a bouquet against the background, thereby obtaining fresher colours than if you were to paint the bouquet directly on to a background, even a pale one.

The brushes used for varnish are simply cleaned in tepid water or spirit.

Many amateur painters have never attempted landscapes as they feel this form of decoration to be beyond them. In our opinion, it is easier to paint a good landscape than a beautiful bouquet. In fact, if the building in a landscape has been clumsily painted, with a little skilfull retouching or the addition of some vegetation it can pass for a romantic ruin. On the other hand, it is very difficult to alter a rose if it looks like a cabbage!

Of course it is useful to have some knowledge of perspective in order to paint a perfect landscape, but beware of producing a mere photograph. It is always preferable to create a landscape with naïve charm rather than one with banal over-accuracy. Remember that painting on china is a part of decorative art, in which all liberties are allowed.

To return to the landscape, let us consider two fundamentally different kinds: first, the complete landscape usually contained in a medallion and secondly, the terraced landscape. In the first case, the landscape is a little picture in itself, completely filling the surface of a cup or the flank of a vase. In the terraced landscape, the foreground is usually composed of foliage and forms a border to the actual terrace supporting the main subject of the landscape such as a building, a group of people, or some birds, in the middle distance. The

◁ It is sometimes difficult to remember the characteristic outline of a particular tree. The illustration on the left will be a helpful reminder. Top row, from left to right: birch, fir and poplar. Middle row: beech and cypress. Bottom row: willow and Scotch pine.

distant background consists of lightly sketched woods or hills. This kind of landscape is very suitable for the middle of a plate or for any lightly decorated piece.

Special attention must be paid to the painting of full, uninterrupted landscapes, because the same rules are easily adapted to the painting of terraced or fragmentary landscapes.

To begin, a balanced landscape must be envisaged and then it must be divided into successive planes. For example, let us take a group of buildings as the principal subject of the landscape. In order not to give them undue importance, place them on a grassy plateau occupying the second or third plane of the picture; the most important feature should never be placed dead centre. A more detailed subject such as a group of trees can be placed on the second plane, in order to re-establish the balance of the picture. Even more detailed features such as rocks, grass and bushes, are worked into the foreground to emphasize the feeling of distance.

Behind the group of buildings, one or two receding 'back-drops' are introduced. Having lightly but carefully drawn these various features, they should now be envisaged as forming superimposed planes, as with stage scenery. Let us begin with the most distant part of the background, in which a mountain range appears. Mix the paint for two separate colours, sky blue and buff-ochre or light ochre. Rapidly follow the outline of the mountains in buff paint, then cover the upper part of the sky in sky-blue, leaving an empty space of ¼ inch between these two colours, which must be kept very pale. Next, with a small skunk-hair stippling brush, dab the buff area until it merges with the unpainted space. Carefully clean the brush and stipple the sky-blue until it touches the buff, thus achieving a beautiful sky with a sparkling golden haze on the horizon. Mix some very pale purplish-grey and fill in the mountains, with a few dark accents to give depth, not forgetting that the source of light is high up on the left.

Continue to paint each successive plane from the background forwards, gradually intensifying the colour and painting each feature in greater detail as you approach the foreground.

The direction of the brushstrokes can give character to a landscape just as it can to a flower. For instance, vertical strokes should be used for the fronts of houses, whereas rooftops should be painted in the direction in which the tiles are hung, and so on.

Among the elements which are essential to the composition of a harmonious landscape, there is one which undoubtedly adds an artistic touch if it is well used; namely, the tree—provided that its character has been thoroughly digested. Some study of the various natural species of trees will obviously help considerably.

We will now briefly describe the characteristics of those trees which are easily integrated into either an uninterrupted or a fragmentary landscape.

THE BIRCH

This tree, with its light airy foliage, is characterised by a pale colouring and drooping clusters of leaves (see page 68, top row, left). The leaves are painted in grey, yellowish-green and moss-green, or yellow, yellowish-green and toast-colour, according to whether the tree is to be shown with its spring or its autumn foliage. Use a long brush (Series 3A, No. 4) and the paints indicated. Paint the leaf clusters in a downward direction, using light touches of paint to form irregular oval dashes gradually diminishing in size and intensity of colour: the foliage is very lacy. The trunk is painted in buff-grey, striated with a few accents of black softened with buff-grey.

THE FIR

There are numerous ways of representing the various species of conifer: we show one which is easy to paint (page 68, top row, middle). Still using the long brush (Series 3A, No. 4), sketch in the trunk with one brisk stroke. The branches and needles are done in the same way: starting from the central axis of the trunk, blackish-green is applied in thin vertical lines which become progressively finer towards the tip of the branch. The tip of the brush always remains in contact with the china, thus emphasizing the rib of the branch in a continuous and slightly arched line. A suggestion of a dead fir or a stump will also add a very artistic touch to a woodland scene.

THE POPLAR

If one observes a poplar in winter, it is easy to see how the numerous branches grow upwards from the trunk, each bearing overhanging branchlets sprouting up towards the sky. The foliage, although very similar in colour and shape to that of the birch, is, on the other hand, drawn in upward growing clusters (page 68, top row, right). The procedure is therefore as with the birch, but reversing the direction of the foliage clusters. The characteristics of this tree are accentuated by a few curved lines lightly sketched in nut-brown; this tree often provides the balancing point in a landscape. A very short piece of the trunk remains visible, as the branches and twigs begin very near the base.

THE BEECH

This is a truly majestic tree, with a well-developed branch system and dense foliage (page 68, middle row, left). Again using the same brush (Series 3 A, No. 4) and yellow, yellowish-green, moss-green and olive-green paint, draw the shape of the tree: its outline is very indented, but the main body is very compact. Then, patches of shadow are made with blackish-green, to suggest the depth of the foliage. To paint a purple beech, with its decidedly decorative characteristics, the same procedure is followed, but using brownish-purple for the first stage and blackish-green for the shading. The trunk, either Y-shaped or with two or three leading branches, stands well clear of the foliage.

THE CYPRESS

With its attenuated shape, it makes a suitable accompaniment to buildings in a landscape of Florentine character and is frequently introduced into the decoration of Paris porcelain. It is very easy to paint (page 68, middle row, right). With the same brush (Series 3 A, No. 4), and using yellow, olive-green and blackish-green, paint irregular shoots partly overlapping each other and leaving only a small part of the trunk visible. None of the branches should show.

THE WILLOW

We suggest the kind of willow that has become misshapen through having its branches cut for use as osiers (page 68, bottom row, left). This tree will fit comfortably beside a pond or on the bank of a river. First paint the knobbly trunk, crowned by one or two protuberances resulting from mutilation. With yellowish-green paint mixed with a little nut-brown, paint some graceful curves to represent the osiers sprouting from these protuberances. Some narrow pointed leaves painted in grey mixed with moss-green will be enough to give this tree its particular individuality.

THE PINE

Each of the numerous varieties of pine has its own characteristics, and it is easy to portray them if one uses one's powers of observation: but we are going to confine ourselves solely to the particularly decorative umbrella pine (page 68, bottom row, right). With toast- and chestnut-browns, paint the twisted and interlacing trunk and main branches. Then, with myrtle-green and blackish-green, make rows of small accents all following the same curved line, and vary the size and intensity of the green patches thus created. The 'umbrella' look of this tree can add a romantic or

The two illustrations show two ways of composing a landscape decoration. Left, the uninterrupted landscape is drawn inside a definite frame and constitutes a small picture in itself. Right, the fragmentary or terraced landscape consists of a very detailed foreground in which is the principal subject; the very lightly painted background fades gradually on the white surface of the china.

even an oriental touch to a landscape, depending on its composition. *Very important general note:* when painting trees in the foreground, the foliage should be firmly and clearly defined; as the trees gradually recede into the background, the painting should be less vigorous and the colours paler, particularly in the outlines.

The importance of this chapter on the various elements of trees could of course be magnified tenfold, but we advise the reader to study nature, either during the period of defoliation in order to master the framework of the tree, or else when it is covered with leaves and their colours and shapes can be absorbed.

SOME ADVICE ON PAINTING BIRDS

Mix all the paints you are going to use for the bird you plan to paint and dilute them sufficiently to produce pastel shades. Spread these colours rapidly one after the other so as to cover the body of the bird completely (brush Series 16, No. 1 or 2). In this way the colours will slightly run into each other; they must not be separated in definite compartments. Take care to spread the paint with small brushstrokes always in the organic direction, which means, following the direction in which the feathers grow.

Once these background colours are thoroughly dry, the ornamentation of the bird is carried out with the same paints as for the background patches, but using great precision in drawing first the large feathers and then the small ones. The scales on the legs and feet and the markings on the beak can be indicated by a few very fine accents in grey-buff mixed with nut-brown. Many other details can be added, depending on the scale and size of the bird, always taking care not to alter its characteristics.

11th EXERCISE
Lines

The gold or coloured line is in some measure the trimming of a piece of china; it gives finish to an object and a frame to the decoration.

Whereas faience or pottery can stand a wavering or irregular line, china is a more precious material and it demands clean-cut precise lines.

It is not necessary to master completely the craft of line drawing in order to trim one's work reasonably well; but adequate tools are indispensable and a few wise rules must be followed.

A turntable is indispensable. It must have a light revolving table so that it can be made to run smoothly. It should have a sliding axis to allow precise setting of the height at which the work can be carried out. The trade supplies a mini-turntable which we do not recommend. It only costs a little less then a workshop turntable, but the problem of setting and the waste of time involved make it in the end a costly and unpractical object.

The line painter's brush is called a liner. It must be thick enough to act as a paint reservoir, as it must enable the painter to draw a completely concentric line with one brushstroke. It is very difficult indeed to draw a perfect line if the operation has to be interrupted to take up a fresh quantity of paint or gold. The first task is to get the object *centred* on the turntable. The professional line painter will achieve this in a few seconds by tapping the object with the top joint of the thumb. A few hours practice will enable you to do the same, or you can try a different procedure. In fact, the revolving table of the turntable is grooved with circles which allow the object to be centred without too much difficulty. Once the piece is centred, the revolving table is set in motion by the successive action of the middle and index fingers of the left hand, the movement being anti-clockwise. The right hand and forearm must lean comfortably against the edge of the table or a supporting shelf.

When dipping the brush in the paint, care must be taken to retain the special shape of the brush. Hold it vertically and perpendicularly to the surface of the object to be lined. With the revolving table now moving, steadily bring the tip of the brush into contact with the piece of china and gradually press it down. At this point, if the brush is held correctly, the hairs will spread fanwise making a sharp edge which should eliminate any slight trembling of the hand and facilitate the drawing of a very neat line.

In order to acquire greater steadiness in starting this exercise, we recommend drawing the line in with a pencil before painting it. In any case, before tackling gold lines we strongly advise you

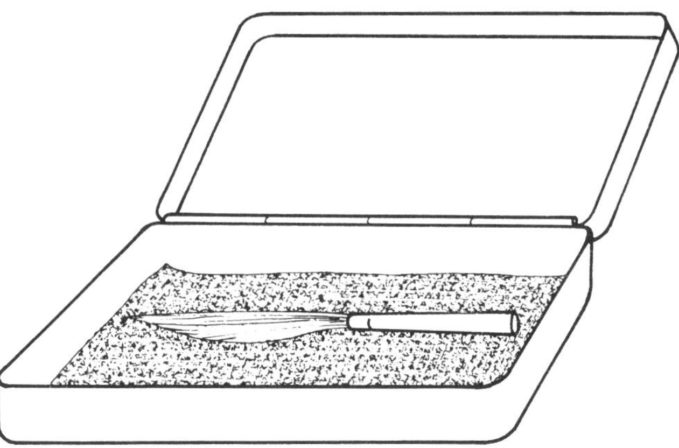

To prevent a cup from moving while you decorate it, weight it down with a lead weight.

Above, right: the slant-cut brush used for gilding is kept in a box provided with a bed of clean material impregnated with medium used for gold. On no account must the brush come in contact with the metal of the box.

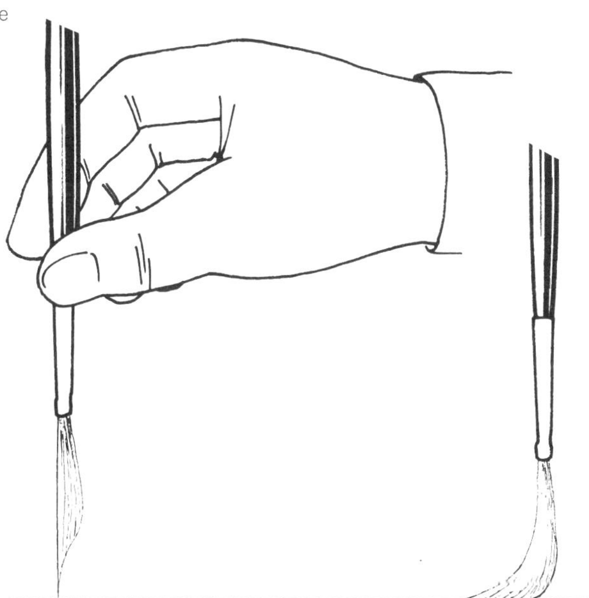

Right: the way to hold and press down the slant-cut brush when painting a hair-line.

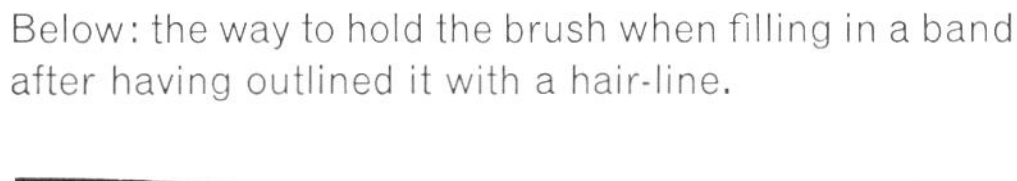

Below: the way to hold the brush when filling in a band after having outlined it with a hair-line.

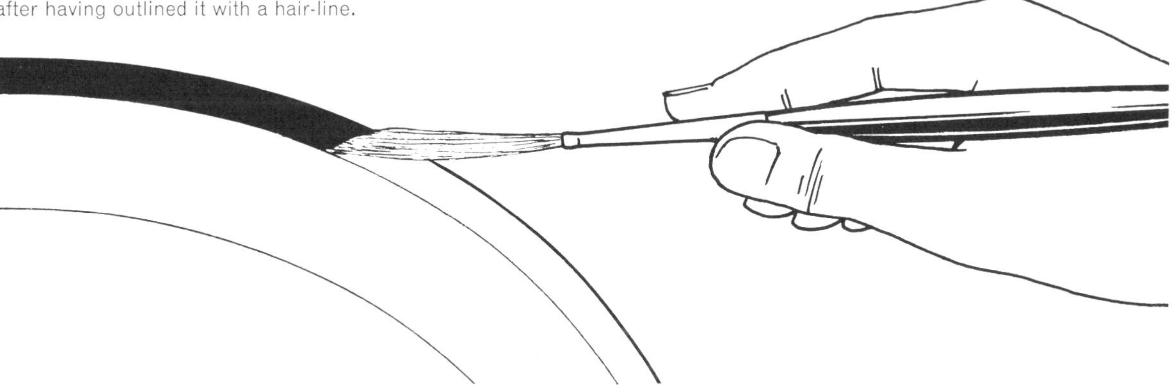

to practise for an hour or two with ordinary paint on an undecorated piece. With this end in view, mix the paint as for the application of a background (with Medium plus oil of cloves).

The position of the brush as shown in the illustration is correct for painting a hair-line, that is to say, a very fine line. As the edge of a plate or other object often needs a band, we will quickly explain how this is done. Where the width of the band has already been marked in pencil, a hair-line is painted over this with the brush held vertically. Then with the same brush, but held almost horizontally, the space between the hair-line and the edge of the piece is filled in with gold or paint. This method will prevent you from letting your brush wander towards the middle of the object, thereby obliging you to make the band disproportionately wider than planned.

As the brush is allowed to 'drag' when painting a band, the surface area in contact with the hairs is considerable, and through adherence there is the risk of de-centering the object on the turntable, especially if it is a small one and therefore light in weight. To counteract this disadvantage, we suggest weighting the object with a ½ lb. lead weight. Old kitchen weights will serve.

By the way, it should be noted that 'preserving' varnish can be used for hair-lines. If, for instance, a band of colour is to be applied to the flange of a plate, it is advisable to draw two lines bordering the area with preserving varnish. This operation is carried out on the turntable with the liner brush. It will then be quite easy to stipple the paint on to the area between the two lines of varnish. When the varnish is removed after the work is finished, the coloured band will have neat clean edges.

And here to end this chapter is a little trick to save time. . . and gold. In order to paint lines properly the brush must be well filled with gold, though not actually dripping. If after each operation the brush is washed to keep it supple, a large quantity of gold is lost. So, as the slant-cut brush is always mounted on a quill and attached to a movable wooden handle, it is easy to separate them and lay the brush itself flat in a small tin box, such as an old pill-box. It should first be lined at the bottom with a pad of clean material which has been soaked in gold medium, because the brush must not come in contact with the metal of the box. In this way the brush will keep its suppleness and will need very little fresh gold the next time it is used.

EXERCISE 12

Imitation inlay, relief and other processes

SIMILI

Real inlay is beyond the scope of the amateur but, nevertheless, thanks to a modern industrial product known as 'simili', interesting results are possible even though they may not produce the same rich effect as real inlay. The characteristic of this technique is that if gold is applied on top of simili it loses part of its brilliance during firing and remains matt in spite of polishing.

Let us take as an example a garland of laurel-leaves on a gold border. The garland, which is to remain matt after firing, is painted with simili, which is mixed in the same way as paint, that is, either with Medium or with the oil and turpentine formula. Simili can be used with a fine paint brush or stippled.

Dip the brush in simili and paint a garland or any other pattern. It is preferable to choose simple patterns, such as leaves or lines, which can be painted in single strokes because simili, unlike paint, cannot be shaded. When the simili has been applied, send the object to be fired. After firing, a coat of gold is applied to the whole of the area to be gilded; use matt gold in preference. After this coat of gold has also been fired, polish the whole pattern. The parts painted in simili (in this case the laurel-leaves) will emerge with a duller surface than where the gold ground has been painted straight on to the white china (see page 78).

GOLD RELIEF

The application of relief makes it possible to embellish cartouches and garlands with raised rococo which is then gilded, thereby considerably enriching the appearance of the object. This technique is not very easy to carry out as its success depends on one very important factor, the mixing of the raising material. The powder used for this must be kneaded for a very long time and only used with oil and turpentine medium: the oil must be in a stronger proportion than when it is used with ordinary paint.

A useful hint: mix in very small doses, just one drop at a time of either oil or turpentine, according to the consistency required. When pulverising the paste, blow on it just as you would to warm your hands. The warmth and moisture of the breath produce an interesting result: the paste becomes firmer and takes on the consistency of thick honey.

It is practical to mix a fairly large amount of paste, using about $^1/_3$ to $^2/_3$ ounce (10 to 20 grammes) of powder; it can be kept in a glass screw-top jar, such as an old face-cream jar. The longer the paste is kneaded and allowed to rest, the greater will its plasticity be. To be of the ideal consistency, it should neither run nor spread on the china. A bead from off the tip of the brush ought to remain almost perfectly round.

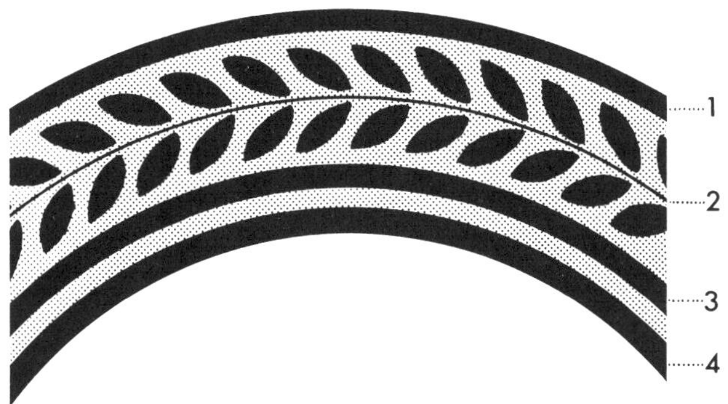

A garland of stylised laurel-leaves lends itself well to imitation inlay. The garland (No. 2) and the lines (Nos. 1, 3 and 4) are painted with simili and will remain matt after polishing the gold. The background (speckled here) will be shiny.

Gilt relief decoration, which involves a difficult technique, is inspired by the delicate designs of the eighteenth century. Geometrical designs are less suited to this type of decoration.

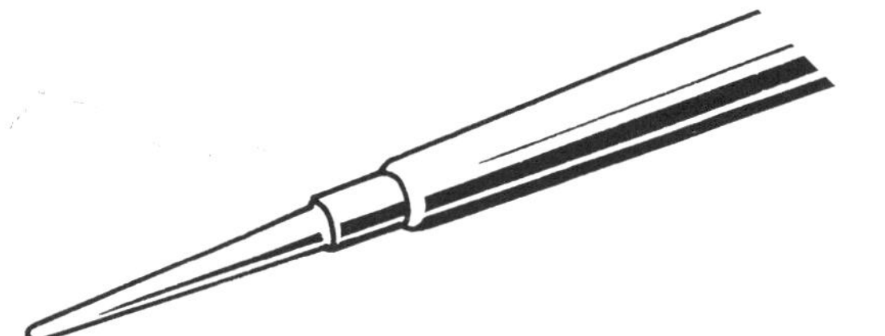

Burnished decoration has the effect of a shiny pattern on a matt gold ground. Geometrical patterns are usually chosen for this type of decoration. A shine is given to a matt gold surface by means of an agate-pointed tool called a burnisher (right).

Laying the raising material is done with a brush (Series 29 A, No. 00 to 2); the difficult part is to assess the amount needed to model a piece of rococo in one brushstroke. Quite high relief can be obtained, but it must not be overdone because of the risk of scaling during firing. After the first firing, apply a coat of matt gold to the relief; then, after a second firing, polish it.

Relief can be used for forming compartments as well as for classical decoration. In this case, rather than a brush, we advise the use of a syringe. A hypodermic syringe with a needle of one millimetre diameter will serve admirably. With this process, a fine, even raised fillet will be obtained, which can be used for surrounding the various colours with a scroll or any other decorative feature.

DECORATION WITH A BURNISHER

This decoration gives the appearance of a brilliant pattern on a background of unpolished matt gold. Burnishing therefore allows an additional decorative feature to be introduced into the gold band around a medallion or the neck of a vase. Geometrical designs lend themselves admirably to this type of decoration.

Burnishing is done with an agate-pointed tool called a burnisher. With light polishing a pattern can be picked out on a matt gold ground which has already been fired. The gold immediately turns shiny wherever the burnisher is applied. When the burnishing is done, wipe the decoration over lightly with a cottonwool pad soaked in oil such as sewing-machine oil (never use cooking oil). The contrast between the burnished or shiny parts and the matt will be heightened by this process.

Although this technique provides wonderful possibilities, it does require a very steady hand. It is not even possible to sketch in the pattern with a pencil, at best one can only use a transfer. Furthermore, this process can only be used with non-utilitarian objects: burnished decoration on a plate or an ash-tray, for instance, will soon be removed by repeated washing and drying. In fact, frequent rubbing on burnished decoration polishes the matt gold surface and makes the whole thing shiny, so that the original pattern disappears.

THE TRANSFER

We will end this section on the technique of painting on china with an account of how to make a transfer.

When the same decorative pattern (such as the lambrequin one of Rouen, for instance) has to be repeated several times on one object or when the pattern is used for a series of objects, rather than drawing it afresh each time, a transfer can be used. This valuable aid is made in the following way: after drawing the pattern in pencil or ink on white paper, trace it with India ink on tracing paper. Then lay this paper on a piece of flannel or other thick material: with a sharp compass point or a needle fixed to a paint brush handle, prick a series of holes close together, keeping exactly to the lines of the pattern. When this is done, turn the tracing over and with very fine sand-paper rub over the tracing, in order to trim the edges of each small hole pricked by the needle. To use this transfer all you have to do is to lay it on the part of the object which you propose to decorate, keeping it in position with a small piece of adhesive tape; then rub the tracing with a pouncing-bag. The latter is easily made: take a piece of fine material 6 sq. in., fill it with a tablespoonful of charcoal powder, gather up the material and tie it together.

After rubbing the pouncing-bag over the tracing, remove the tracing carefully from the china. The pattern will then appear in black dotted lines. As this filigree pattern is very fragile and can disappear at a touch, it is advisable to strengthen it with a few pencil marks before starting to paint it.

ADVICE AND SUGGESTIONS

THE FIRST OBJECTS

You will have noticed that for your first exercises with cornflowers and other all-over flower designs we advised using a plain plate of 7 ½ to 10 inches diameter as a 'trial ground', because a smooth simple shape does of course make it easier to carry out a harmoniously scattered flower design. But as it would be tedious always to use the same shape, it is obvious that you will now want to give expression to your talent by painting pieces more suited to your taste and needs. At this stage we would like to issue a warning which we consider important: after your first successful ventures, do not immediately plunge into the decoration of a whole service, whether it be a dinner, tea or coffee one. Indeed, although the first plates you paint will seem perfect to you and will fire you with enthusiasm, you will continue to make progress if you just keep on practising. As your brushstrokes and your eye improve, you will regret having painted a whole service too soon in what will later seem to you a clumsy fashion. We would remind you that our method of instruction bears fruit all the quicker with constant practice. So do not hesitate to rub out work which does not give you entire satisfaction, and curb your impatience when your instinct is to send a seemingly perfect piece to be fired. Wait a day or two, and you are sure to find some imperfection which had at first escaped your notice.

In order to develop your skill and your sense of decoration, we advise you to tackle objects of varied shape and avoid the pitfall of the miniature piece. To get good results a certain surface area is necessary; moreover, a beginner rarely succeeds when the scale of the work is much reduced and a small piece may look ridiculous if overloaded with too heavy a decoration. When putting the first lessons into practice we would therefore advise painting a few simple objects to start with, such as a butter-, flan-, or cake-dish, and then progressing to pieces with more difficult shapes such as tumblers, cream-jugs, small vases and cups. Here you will be faced with new problems; not only will the placing of the ornamentation be a test of your decorative sense, but the manipulation of an object of volume, rather than one with a flat surface such as a plate, will add to your difficulties. The object must indeed be held very delicately in the left hand, taking care not to touch the decoration with the fingers. The hand holding the brush only comes in contact with the china if there is no elbow-rest; so it is important, right from the first exercise, to get used to using the tip of the little finger only by way of support. Let us here digress for a moment to note that each finished object must be minutely examined before firing because, although spots of gold can be easily removed after firing by means of a special abrasive rubbing eraser, it is almost impossible to remove spots of paint. There are also other kinds

◁ This bath-salts jar (opposite) is very pretty and effective; the lozenges are gold, and inside them are roses, rosebuds and forget-me-nots.

This coffee-set combines garlands of small flowers with wavy ribbons (detail above). With this design it is difficult to arrange the pattern artistically round the cup. Care must be taken to avoid a heavy look, by balancing the size of the pattern with the dimensions of the cup.

This plate (left), despite its apparent simplicity, is a little more difficult. Before starting, one must have completely mastered the technique of the small bunch. Similar designs are found in the decoration of Old Paris china. The border is in raised gilt rococo and calls for a steady hand.

A very fine example (right) of scattered multi-floral decoration, ▷ which is the result of Exercises 3 to 5. The border is in 'dog's-teeth' pattern as described on pp. 48 and 51. These delicate little flowers must be scattered harmoniously over the whole of the available surface. When in doubt, make a sketch on paper the same size as the object.

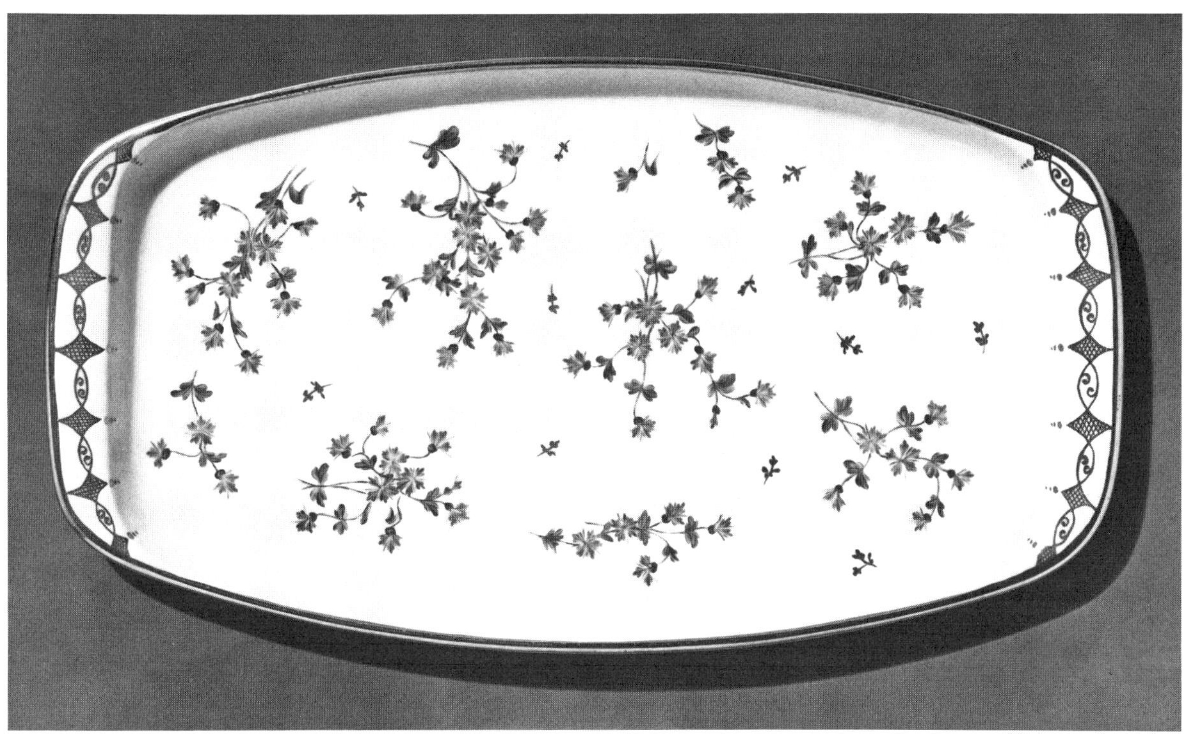

◁ The cup and saucer on the left is painted in monochrome. The design, which at one time was widely used in Saxony, has a charmingly rustic look. When painting a monochrome design, the modelling of the various parts of the pattern must be very thorough.

This cake-tray is easy to paint for anyone who has practised drawing bunches of cornflowers. Leaves and flowers must be very delicately painted to give an effect of lightness. The gold border presents no particular problem.

of marks which are hard to detect before firing: the marks made by perspiring hands. Experience has proved that if the hand holding the object touches the same place for several minutes, a little perspiration is deposited on the china and can make ugly greyish patches during firing, which are indelible. It is therefore advisable to clean thoroughly all undecorated surfaces with a small wad of clean material soaked in spirit.

To return to some articles which will enable you to try your hand as a beginner without too much trouble, we suggest some which are both useful and decorative such as ash-trays, pin-trays, candy-dishes and flower-vases. To give a personal touch to a kitchen, a bowl or two, mugs, pans, a salad-bowl or spice-jars will do nicely. For the garden, a set of lemonade jug and glasses or ice-cream cups; or there are charming small ink-pots and pen-holders in either modern or period style for a man's writing-desk. The bathroom also provides endless opportunities to show off your talent, such as tooth-mugs, soap-dishes, powder-boxes, jars for bath-salts and scent-bottles. A well-furnished dining-table can also provide surprises for your guests; even before you feel competent to greet them with a complete dinner-service decorated by yourself, you can make a start with various small decorative pieces such as salt-cellars, mustard-pots, finger-bowls, bread-baskets and so on.

To ornament this bowl, the painter has combined two relatively simple patterns, the trellis and the bouquet. Elegance is imparted by harmonising the colours with the two most important flowers, the marguerite and the convolvulus. The background of the trellis pattern must be kept very soft and light in colour.

FIRST PRESENTS

A great deal of practice is essential if you wish to make rapid progress, and you will soon litter your house with a multitude of utilitarian or decorative objects which you will have painted with ever-increasing skill. But do not worry, for you will never reach a saturation point, as is alas the case with certain other hobbies. Two ways are open to you, if you wish to avoid being invaded by a mass of objects for which you have no use and still continue to practise your painting. The first way is to erase your work after each practice. But perhaps this is bad for morale, and it would be a pity to lose the enthusiasm which painting on china inevitably arouses. What is the other solution? Give presents! You will very soon notice that your friends and

No pipe-smoker can resist a tobacco-jar, particularly if it is a present from the artist. When choosing the shape and decoration, avoid anything which may look finicky. This eighteenth century tobacco-jar (above, right) could serve as a model, or a simple pattern like this one on the left could be copied. The word 'tobacco' in particular must have a solid appearance, and fragile-looking letters must be avoided; the whole piece should look attractively masculine.

guests will be amazed by your unsuspected talent and you can be sure that their congratulations will be sincere. You are the only one who is going to know that a particular piece of decoration is not perfect, or that some small fault could have been avoided, because as your skill increases you will become progressively exacting regarding your own work. These small faults will be indiscernible to people who have never done any painting on china, unless they happen to be real experts, which is unlikely. So take advantage of your visitors' admiration for some object and see what pleasure you will give them (and yourself) by presenting them with the admired piece on some special occasion. The person to whom you give a piece of your handiwork is certain to honour you by placing a special order, for instance a whole tea-set or coffee-set of which you have given one cup. You will have almost become a professional! Accept all orders, even if the material profit is minimal or even nil, because it is a worthwhile opportunity to increase your proficiency, while at the same time reducing your costs. You will moreover be surprised to find that your works not only arouse admiration, but also curiosity; people will ask you if it is difficult, and how you set about it. Never hesitate to offer help to a potential painter on china: you will suddenly realise that you have become an art teacher! If you agree to hand on your knowledge to an interested person,

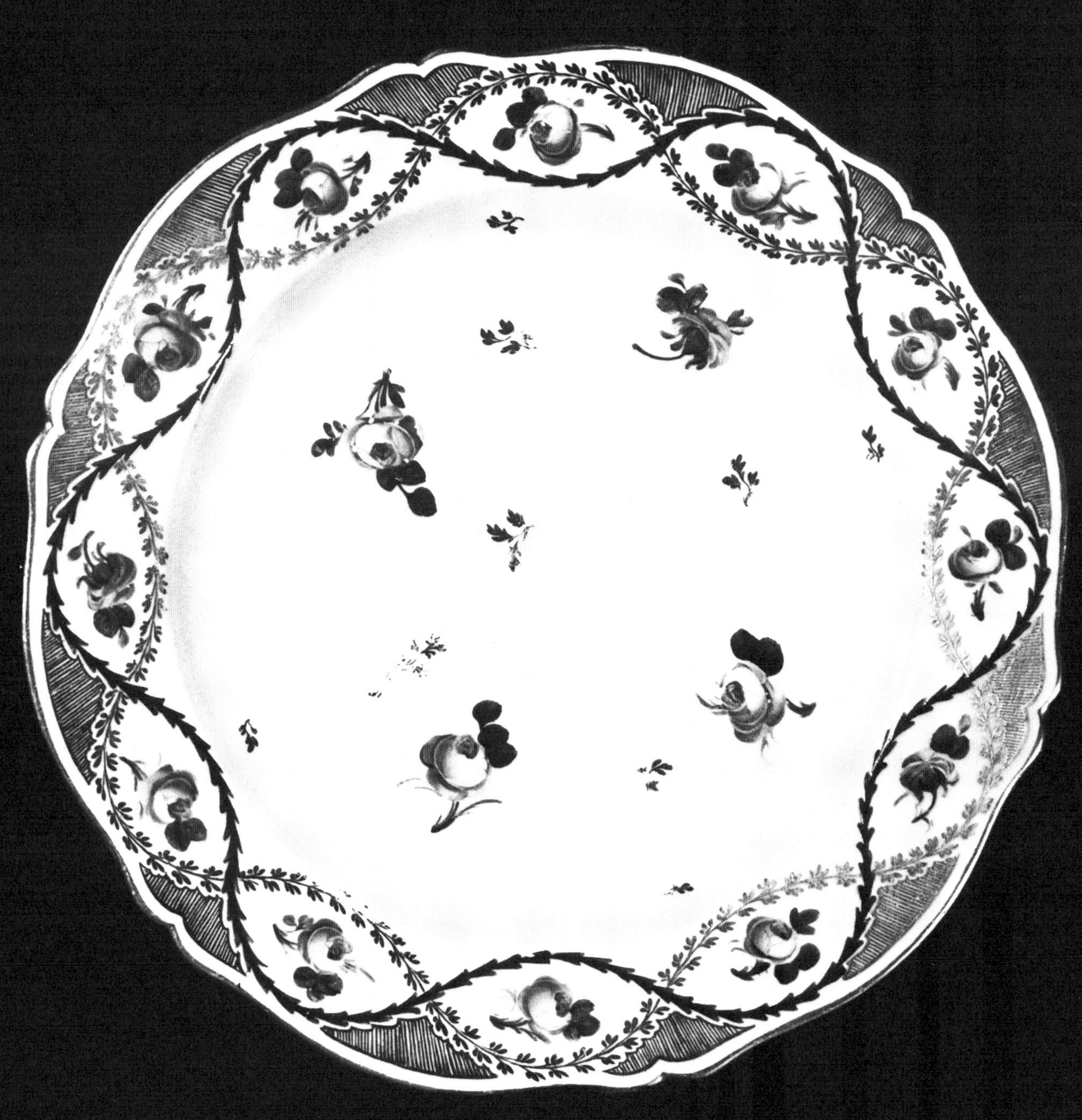

◁ This plate (left) with interlacing decoration, hatching and scattered roses, is a little more difficult. It shows the influence of the Sèvres and Limoges factories. It is important that the pattern of roses in the middle of the plate should not be too obviously geometrical. And take care to make your roses look like roses, and not cabbages!

The monogram (below) is the most noteworthy part of this service. The decoration consists of a garland of polychrome flowers linked with blue urns and bordered with a blue and gold ovum pattern. These pieces are redolent of the grace and elegance of the French eighteenth century. The monogram in the middle of the plate gives the present a more personal touch; this set was ordered by Madame Du Barry.

The antique snuff-box (right) is used nowadays as a pin-tray, ▷ sweet-box or even a match-box. This one is decorated with vine-leaves and grapes, a pleasant design which can be stylised or not, according to taste.

Everything in nature inspires the imagination of the painter on china. This little set, consisting of a salt-cellar, a small pot, an egg-cup, a mustard-pot and a large covered bowl, is decorated with twigs. A walk in the garden or the fields produces endless ideas for decoration of this kind; a certain stylisation, together with grace and a light touch, is essential.

you will not fail to derive surprising benefit from this initiation process: the mere fact of having precisely to explain a brushstroke or the light and shade of a flower will make your own work more careful and neat. On the other hand, as all tastes differ, you may find that your pupil's interpretation includes some idea worthy of development or exploitation. It may seem paradoxical, but a great deal can be learned from a pupil. But let us return to the joy of giving. There are endless possibilities, not only in the choice of decoration, but also in the selection of shapes because present-day china manufacturers offer a wide range of pieces which show good taste and are very suitable for decoration. So it is up to you to use discernment and imagination when making your choice. Whereas a decoration of flowers, either scattered or in bunches, almost always pleases a woman, it is not the same for a man, who will want something more robust but still elegant, if somewhat less delicate. With a little ingenuity, you will be able to introduce some favourite sport, in a way which is elegant or even humorous, or allude to some small idiosyncrasy. The problem is quickly solved for a smoker, as ash-trays, tobacco-jars, pipe-racks and table lighters are always appreciated. As for the inveterate smoker, he will always be amused by a witty inscription on his tobacco-jar based on the Latin ones on old pharmacy jars,

This terrine is ornamented with garlands of cornflowers interspersed with roses. The decoration is Dutch and is a little more naturalistic than that of Nyon. The charm of this pattern lies in the subtle balance between flowers and foliage.

Right: this eighteenth century butterfly service in the Nyon manner is light, gay and original. You could well take your inspiration from it, and either find living models for the butterflies or take them from illustrations in old books on entomology. ▷

which are most effective: for instance 'Extr. Opii.', 'Extr. Cannabis Ind.' (or hashish), 'Nicotiana Tabacum', etc. For the usual objects to be found on a man's desk we suggest a more sober decoration, such as a cypher with interlacing initials in gold and one other colour. For someone romantically inclined, a landscape is more attractive. Pictures of old sailing-ships or old maps would be suitable for a man who is keen on travel and adventure and vintage cars, although a well-worn theme, are certain to be a success with an automobile enthusiast.

There is a vast choice of presents for a woman, the undoubted favourite being the flower-vase. Whether it is a small vase to place in front of each guest on the dining-table, a tall vase to hold a single orchid, or a large one for a sumptuous bouquet, the decoration of this kind of vase should never be so heavy that it detracts from the charm of the flowers. On the other hand, a purely decorative piece such as an Empire vase with swan-neck handles can stand very elaborate decoration; also, this kind of vase can almost always be turned into a lamp. Lamps are greatly appreciated and the trade supplies them in many different shapes and sizes, such as bedside lamps, dressing-table lamps, reading lamps etc. Every kind of decoration can be used, from the most

The decoration of this rectangular dish or tray is a good example of the full, uninterrupted landscape: it is painted in brown monochrome. The subject represents the romantic ruins so popular during the last century. The border is in gold.

◁ Flowers have given place to birds on this cup and saucer (left). When painting a similar subject, the shape, position and colour of the birds must harmonise to form a pleasing whole. To avoid any disappointment, it is essential to make a preliminary study on paper.

conventional to the most fantastic. Take care, however, to choose a shape with a wide enough base to give the lamp sufficient stability.

For a christening present, give a hot-water plate, a shallow bowl-shaped porridge plate, or a bowl with handles. Decorate with pictures taken from nursery rhyme illustrations, and it will give great pleasure. Avoid using gold, because children have more natural appreciation of bright colours. For a little girl one suggestion is to give tea-cups or coffee-cups, adding something on each birthday until you have made up a complete set, to which you can later add cake-dishes and bread-and-butter plates.

There is nothing to stop you trying your hand at Japanese decoration. This plate with very stylised foliage is a good example and could be a starting-point. Patterns can be chosen from old prints or illustrated books. It should be remembered that the most beautiful Japanese designs are often, if not always, the simplest.

Nowadays, when house-plants are so popular, a pot-holder is a greatly appreciated present. Choose rather less detailed decoration than for table china. Flowers or landscapes must suit the shape of the pot.

A pretty bunch on the bulge of this teapot is enough to give it a well-bred look, proving that it is unnecessary to add pointless complications to the design. It is more important that the pattern be well adapted to the volume and shape of the object.

The decoration of this cup and saucer (below) is carried out entirely in gold. It was made at Derby between 1785 and 1790, and it could serve as model for a complete service. But this type of work demands great regularity in the design; if necessary, this can be achieved by using a transfer.

The Chinese decoration of this Meissen teapot (right) dates from the beginning of the eighteenth century and is more elaborate than that on page 97. To be perfect, each piece of the tea-set should have a different picture, but in the same style and range of colours.

WORK FOR THE EXPERIENCED PERSON

As previously explained, we recommend constant practice of the exercises we describe before embarking on tasks which call for wide experience. If you progress gradually to more demanding work you will find that the skill will come almost automatically.

Before taking on a complicated piece of work, an unusual piece, or a whole service, it is a good idea to make a definite plan of the work to be done. Let us take for example a vase with a coloured background and a medallion with a flower design. First, cover the surface of the medallion or cartouche with reserving varnish, then apply the background colour and send the

piece to be fired. A second application and a second firing are necessary for a dark colour such as Empire green or rich purple. The second phase includes the flower decoration, the gold surrounding the medallion and, lastly, the gold handles. As gold applied on top of colour will certainly need retouching, take the opportunity to put some shading on the flowers, then fire at a lower temperature (maximum 1320 degrees Fahrenheit). When decorating a whole service, certain precautions are indispensable: enough paint must be mixed to avoid interrupting the work in order to re-mix, because it is vital to apply the background to all the pieces at the same time. In this way the colour is more likely to be identical on each piece. One word of advice: always keep the first piece on which you have stippled the background in sight, and it will enable you to keep a check on the depth of colour of each subsequent piece as you paint it. Let us take a different example: the 'Queen of Naples' decoration on page 101 is carried out in two stages. First, paint the gold lines of the border; once the gold is dry, still using gold, paint the rings between the lines together with the garlands, and send it to be fired. The second stage consists of filling in the black parts of the border and in retouching the gold, which will almost certainly be necessary.

If the trade can produce some of the plain white shapes similar to those of the eighteenth century, one could copy this pattern of fruit and trellis made at Kloster Veilsdorf. The central motif alone could also be used to decorate a plate of modern design. Here again, the central motif should be different on each plate, in order to avoid a monotonous effect.

When the principal decorative theme of a service like the one shown on page 102 is repeated on each piece, it is advisable to adapt the size and outline of each bouquet to the shape and dimensions of the object. Notice how the bouquet on the coffee-pot has been skilfully elongated vertically whereas it has been extended horizontally on the ample bulge of the teapot. The additional small sprigs on the flange of the plate and the upper parts and lids of the larger pieces help to attenuate the contrast between a mass of flowers and a blank area. To achieve complete success with this kind of decoration, one must take care to vary the composition of each bunch; this will have the added advantage of developing your imagination and your aesthetic sense.

The decoration of the hand-bell shown on page 103 is a good example of the look of freshness and distinction which is so attractive. This light and airy decoration can also be used for cups; the garlands composed of delicately drawn flowers trail from a compact lattice bordered by lightly raised rococo. The charm of this design lies in the contrast between the two elements; but to obtain a similar result, the lattice must be faultlessly painted.

The water-jug shown on page 104 is a wonderful example of what can be done with this apparently banal shape; a seascape, treated like a terraced landscape and very artistically composed, encircles its bulge. Notice that the principal subject of the foreground is not placed centrally, but that its position near the handle seems to integrate the handle with the decoration. You will certainly have noticed the unlikely presence of insects and tiny flowers above the landscape; this fanciful feature is certainly not introduced deliberately into the design, but is a cunning way of camouflaging a defect in the glazing. These defects are seen less and less often nowadays. Here is proof

A tea-set with garlands and a border in the Nyon manner. There is another example of this design on page 40. The pattern is very light and marries perfectly with the elegant shapes of the service. This motif is known as the 'Queen of Naples' pattern.

A small china hand-bell is rarely used today, as electricity has replaced it. Treated as a decorative object, it is simply used to mark the place at table of the lady of the house. This little bell belonged to the Prussian General von Möllendorf in about 1765.

Bunches of flowers copied from eighteenth century examples decorate the various pieces of a combined tea- and coffee-set (left). Each piece has a different motif, but one could quite well paint all the pieces of one series alike. Designs could be taken from the examples shown on pp. 39, 49, and 57.

Water-jugs and crocks often have a rather heavy bulging shape, which does not go well with flowers. The Dutch artist who painted this jug chose a seascape such as those portrayed in pictures of the time. Why not use similar decoration for some of the objects in a country house?

that a fault can always be rectified by clever decorating and can even be turned into a feature.

Page 105 shows a typical example of a decoration which covers the whole surface of the object but still retains a look of remarkable lightness. The artist has painted a series of small bunches at regular intervals, linked by a network of wavy ribbons intertwined with airy sprays. The effect is one of tapestry which, despite its regularity of design, is threaded with freshness and fantasy. To obtain this effect we advise the following procedure: start by marking the places for all the little bunches with a pencil and then, leaving these places blank, sketch in the ribbons with a long brush in a pastel colour, and send the piece to be fired. Second stage: paint the small bunches and also the intertwining sprays and, with a few deft touches, shade the ribbons.

Page 106 shows a tea-caddy decorated with fruit, which is most unusual for a piece of this kind. The composition of a fruit design is based on the same lines laid down for a flower pattern. Choose some fruit of different sizes, cutting some in half, and arrange them in a harmonious group. As in the case of the tea-caddy, a few branchlets bearing smaller fruit are necessary to give lightness to the decoration, which might otherwise look rather heavy. A few nuts, either whole or broken, are used to balance the composition, as in a still-life. One other thing is worth mentioning: whereas flowers are never shown casting a shadow, with a collection of fruit this is essential as it gives the whole group a look of stability, without which the fruit would seem to be floating in space. A butterfly and other insects add a lively touch to decoration which can, if treated unimaginatively, look merely

Both the shapes and the pattern of this Nymphenburg service are most distinctive; it is a museum piece. A decorator who appreciates objects of beauty and is an expert with the paint brush might well use this design as a model.

People who appreciate a certain restraint in the decoration of table china could emulate this plate (above), painted at Frankenthal for a princess. The decoration is in purplish red monochrome, with only the monogram in gold.

This plate (right) could serve as a model for a whole fish-service; the fish itself is painted in subtle shades, whereas the border is in gold. Of course the set could be improved by painting a different fish on each plate, either fresh-water or deep-sea varieties. They can be copied from old prints or from the identification plates published for fishermen and fish shops.

A well-placed naturalistic design distinctly improves the rather banal appearance of this tea-caddy (left).

dull and ordinary. Do not make too large a quantity of this china; at the most, a tea-set or a breakfast-set will be enough not to be overpowering. Also on page 106 we show a beautiful example of a cyphered plate, with a monogram on the flange combined with flower decoration of a particular kind: a single stem of flowers and leaves, occupying the centre of the plate with a continuous garland surrounding the edge. To link these two features, the artist has used small scattered flowers in an ingenious way. The size of the flowers diminishes as they gradually get nearer the middle, thereby attenuating the impact of the central motif. The elegance of these scattered flowers lies as much in the detailed execution as in the irregularity of the disposition. The monogram is discreetly integrated with the pattern. You may perhaps wish to decorate a set of fish-plates and dishes? The plate shown on page 107 is an excellent example of a service of this kind; the straightforwardness of the drawing makes the fish look like an illustration from a treatise on ichthyology. This style is by far the most effective; if the fish were accompanied by seaweed and bubbles floating in blue ripples the design would lose all its decorative quality and become merely commonplace. On the other hand seaweed has been used in masterly fashion to form a very decorative garland with little groups of coral and shells at intervals. This kind of fish picture is not at all

The Japanese decoration of this plate painted at Meissen in about 1730 is an excellent example of stylisation. The bird is quite definitely a bird, the flowers are flowers, and the leaves are leaves; but it would be very hard to give specific names to any of them. Let us once again repeat, painting on porcelain is an interpretation, not a reproduction, of reality.

The lesson to be learned from this polychrome flower-decorated jar and lid is in the use of the available surface and the choice of design. Garlands of flowers or small bunches would not have suited the bulging shape of the jar. The pattern chosen is in perfect harmony; it is placed neither too high nor too low, and it gives the jar the true distinction of a work of art. ▷

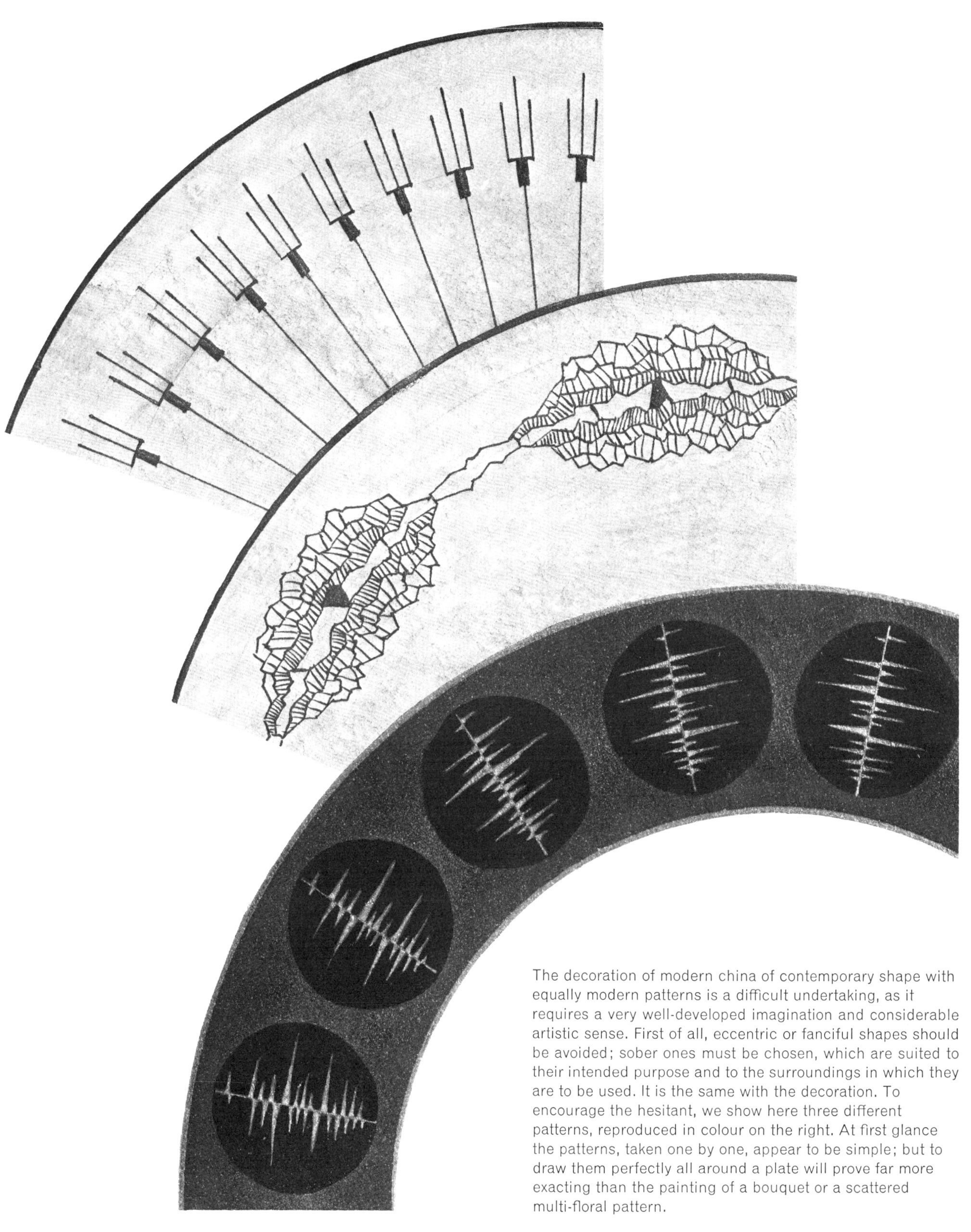

The decoration of modern china of contemporary shape with equally modern patterns is a difficult undertaking, as it requires a very well-developed imagination and considerable artistic sense. First of all, eccentric or fanciful shapes should be avoided; sober ones must be chosen, which are suited to their intended purpose and to the surroundings in which they are to be used. It is the same with the decoration. To encourage the hesitant, we show here three different patterns, reproduced in colour on the right. At first glance the patterns, taken one by one, appear to be simple; but to draw them perfectly all around a plate will prove far more exacting than the painting of a bouquet or a scattered multi-floral pattern.

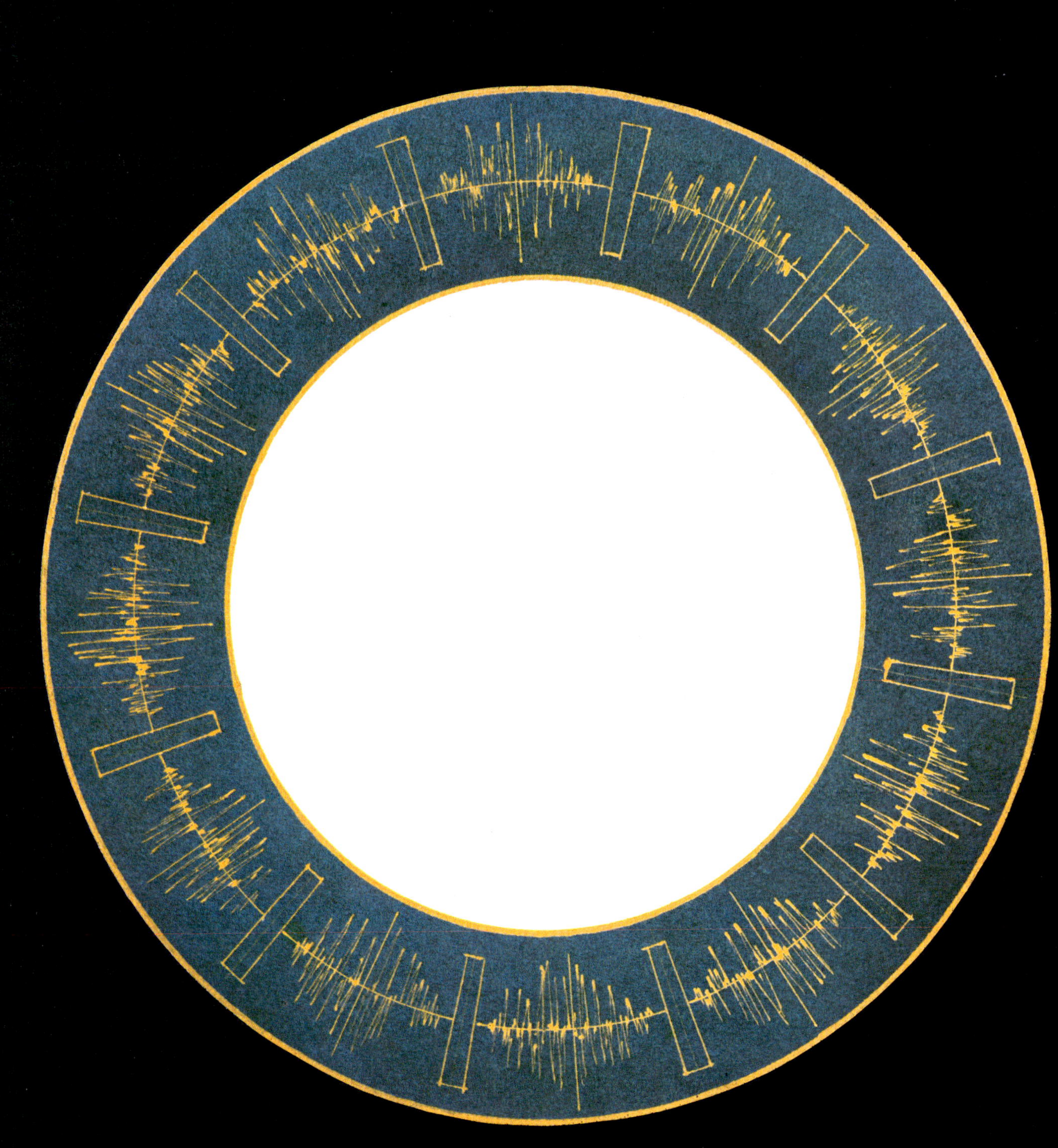

◁ This example of contemporary decoration is inspired by scientific features typical of our age (left). It shows a new way of using present-day phenomena which, through electronic processes, often take the form of oscillations. The economy of colour—a blue and a gold—in no way detracts from the well-bred overall effect.

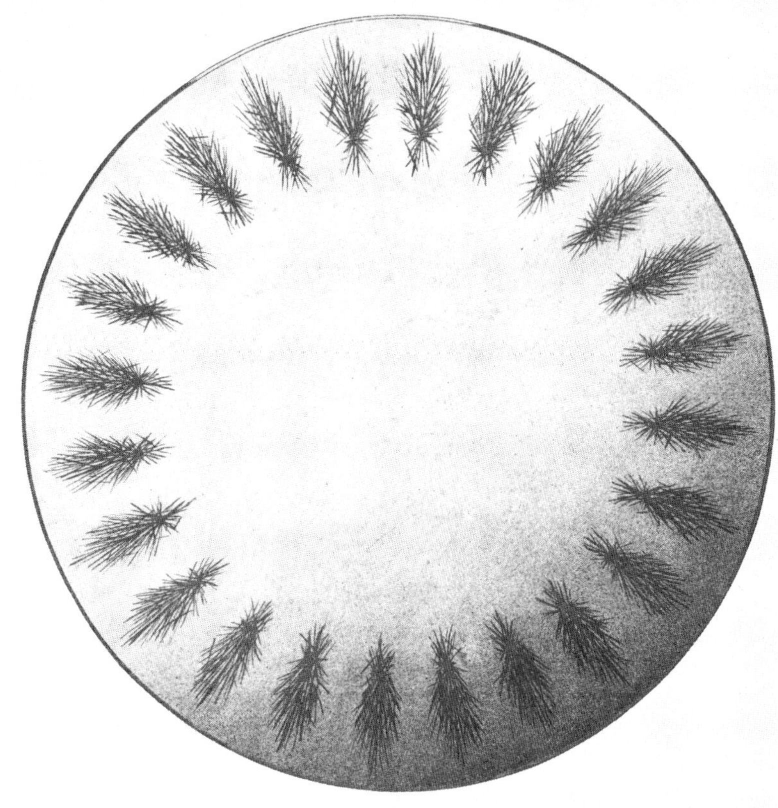

Bundles of twigs arranged in a circle around the edge of the plates and other pieces of this service are reminiscent of the trophies of the eighteenth century (right). Painted in gold on a single colour background, the decoration is very distinctive, in spite of its simplicity. It looks most impressive on a suitable tablecloth.

easy to draw. Here we would like to mention another fish design, produced by the Marseilles workshop of the Widow Perrin about 1760. It features trophies, in which fish of all kinds are piled up in a rich jumble of colours, some of them lying on a bed of seaweed, draped in fishing-nets and accompanied by baskets of sea-urchins. In this kind of decoration, the arrangements of fish, sea-food, crustacea and fishing-tackle can be varied indefinitely. In our opinion, this is one of the best ways to decorate a fish-service. But perhaps you are not attracted by period decoration and your taste is more drawn towards abstract designs or at any rate something more contemporary. Of course there is nothing to prevent you designing your own original patterns, original both in colour and form. All the same, we would like to repeat two fundamental maxims: 1) never forget that your china objects must have a certain staying power, because they are made to last and you should never become tired of them; 2) painting a repeating abstract pattern does not allow for any smudging or hesitation, because the effect of the decoration would be ruined. To divide a plate into equal parts, we advise you to refer to the diagram at the end of this book, on page 124. With the help of a tracing, you can place your motifs exactly in the positions which they are to occupy. On pp. 110 to 112 and above, you will find some suggested contemporary decorations: if you use them as references and starting-points, you will avoid making regrettable mistakes. If you are cautiously forward-looking your pieces will give you lasting pleasure and they will indeed be a joy to the friends who visit you to share your hours of leisure.

Nowadays pieces of faience are very popular when they are decorated in a naïve rustic style. But this does not mean that some of them are not beautiful, as can be seen in these two pieces of Iznik pottery from Turkey (above). Stylisation and bold patches of well-chosen colour produce a harmonious relationship between the object and the decoration.

This dish of Rhodes faience, with a 'lambrequin' border, is decorated with very stylised flowers which are somewhat reminiscent of the patterns in certain oriental carpets. The flower decoration is painted in several colours, more for the effect than for a faithful adherence to nature. The same pattern could well be carried out in monochrome.

PAINTING ON FAIENCE

The decoration of faience is carried out by means of two different techniques: these are the hard-fired process (1650 to 1850 degrees F.), which is the oldest method, and the soft-fired process, or firing in a muffle kiln. The second is a relatively recent method used at the time of the birth of European porcelain, that is, at the beginning of the eighteenth century. The decorating is done with the same on-glaze paint which is used for porcelain, but with faience the firing temperature is no higher than 1320 degrees F., as opposed to 1480 degrees F. for porcelain.

For hard-fired decoration, the most widely used and, today, the most easily accessible technique is under-glaze painting. It is done with paints containing no vitrifiable matter, which are soluble in water and are applied to unglazed white faience. Before firing, the object thus decorated is covered with a thin coat of transparent glaze which will render it waterproof and fix the colours. This technique produces very beautiful effects, but it calls for a much bolder style. So one must rather forget about china and its precious nature, and emphasize the rustic charm of faience. Page 114 shows some wonderful examples, two ancient faiences from Iznik and a dish from Rhodes. The stylised, well-balanced decoration is spread over the whole surface of the object; it can also be applied to glazed china, by using the paints mixed according to the method we have described. One should not hesitate to apply a distinctly thicker coat of paint than on china, as the risk of the paint flaking after firing is practically non-existent. The rustic art which is peculiar to the folklore of every country provides hundreds of ideas which can be adapted to suit any piece of faience. One of the most interesting objects is the wall-tile, as much for its cheapness as for the many different uses to which it can be put. It is supplied by the trade in standard sizes of 4, 6 and 8 square inches. When framed, these tiles make delightful small pictures; set in brass or wrought iron, they are much appreciated as table-mats; or, used in a group of four or six, they can form the base of a tray. They can also be used to cover the top of a low table for serving drinks. And indeed why should they not be decorated and used for their original purpose, which is as wall-covering? So here is a chance to enliven the walls of your kitchen or bathroom with a very personal touch—and cause envy all round! On pages 116 and 117 are shown some illustrations of old tiles made in European factories for North African palaces. Each of these tiles forms one quarter of a decorative feature, and you can easily visualise the effect of a complete pattern by holding two mirrors to the corners of one of these tiles. There is another suggestion on page 122, where the decoration is spread over the whole surface of the wall without any repeat of the pattern. For this scheme, we advise you to number each tile on the back to facilitate hanging, unless you have a special passion for jig-saw puzzles!

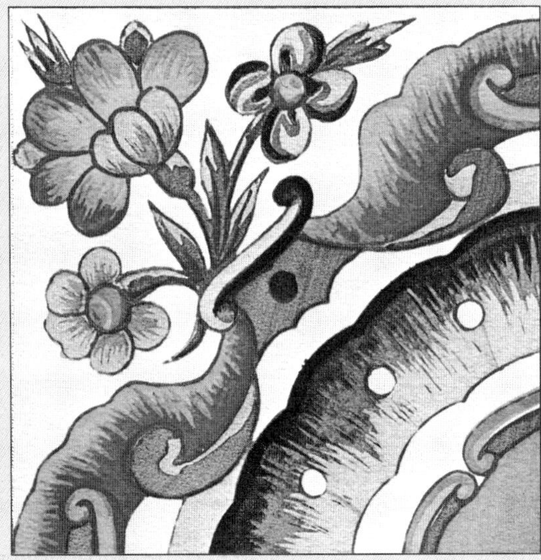

In spite of the increasing use of commercially produced tiles, hand-decorated ones still have a fascination for many amateurs. The pattern chosen should suit the purpose to which the tiles are to be put. Left, three Italian designs found in houses in North Africa.

Rustic scenes painted on faience with a few strokes of the brush are a quick easy way of giving expression to your imagination, but it should not be forgotten that faience can also be the medium for elaborate decoration. Before porcelain appeared in Europe, the makers of faience set themselves to create decoration of remarkable quality and they attained perfection in their craft. In France we need only mention the landscapes of the Marseilles factory, the grotesques of Moustiers, the lambrequin patterns of Rouen, and the flower painting of Sceaux, Meillonas and Strasbourg. Well-known painters such as Joseph Hannong developed flower painting on faience to perfection. Nevertheless, we strongly advise you not to try and adapt to faience the style you have learned from our method of painting on china. Without making the decoration too heavy, you can afford to paint with a much fuller brush, and use stronger and more vigorous colours than you have done on china. We suggest a style which will soon make this technique clear to you, which is known as the *chatironné* technique; it was used in masterly fashion at Strasbourg and Lunéville. The expression comes from the German verb *schattieren*, to shade, or give a shadow to; what is really meant is to 'make a ring round', or outline, the main features. But this outlining must be delicately done, with downstrokes and up-strokes, both full and slender, as practised in fine calligraphy; the decoration must

To decorate tiles, two different techniques can be used conjointly: evenly spreading a flat tint or wash, and shading afterwards. In this way, a design is built up formed by several tiles, and the effect is considerably enlivened by shading. Top and bottom, Italian designs; middle, a design from Moustiers.

not be divided into compartments by a line of uniform thickness resembling a strand of wire. We advise the following procedure: first paint flowers and leaves with bold brushstrokes; when dry, proceed with the *chatironnage*, or shadowing, which is done in black (see page 121).

We repeat that this work needs a light touch: the gracefulness of the various elements must be emphasized by finely-drawn lines, together with some hatching for the shading. Do not make the mistake of starting with your outlining because, not only is it illogical, but the work of filling-in which would have to follow would inevitably encroach on the first lines; moreover, the fact of being confined to a definite area by an outline would deprive your painting of all freedom and gusto. Furthermore, the system of filling-in an outline is a childish art not suited to the decoration in question. The finish of a piece of faience must not be treated in the same way as that of china. Gold is of course the trimming of china and gives it the character of something precious, akin to the goldsmith's work; but it looks wrong on faience. Although faience can also reach a high level of quality, by the very nature of its material—its solidity and its thick glaze—it calls for decoration in which beauty and freshness spring from modesty.

Although a gold line and borders of sprays, rococo and garlands add to the beauty of china, unfortunately they give faience a flashy look which

The Dutch are past-masters in the art of painting tiles; their designs are always taken from nature or from scenes of everyday life. They used blue with great skill, but were never averse to greens, yellows, and red for flower patterns.

can ruin a carefully thought-out design. A line of colour, either a single one or one which is combined with 'combing' or 'feathering', or rococo, will always provide a finish which is appropriate. It can either be painted in the dominant colour of the central motif, or in a completely contrasting one; in any case there is little risk of making a mistake, as faience can take bright, almost violent colours with great ease. It is a material in which you can make pieces look old, if you like antiques, and you may choose to accentuate the 'period' look by giving it a patina. Thus, the relief pattern of an object can be emphasized with a light coating of artificial dirt in the hollows, or else the whole surface can be covered with a thin uneven skin. This process can be used either hot or cold; applied hot, it will give a certain matt look to the piece and a patina which almost has the authentic 'old' appearance. To do this, quickly spread over the whole surface of the object a solution which is made as follows: dissolve Judean bitumen with gasoline or benzine and wipe the surface with a soft rag before it is dry. Although this process gives good results, it has one disadvantage: the object thus treated can never be used for the table because washing removes the patina. There remains the hot process which necessitates a second firing. It is as follows: mix some dark brown paint, such as Van Dyck brown, in the same way as for a background; spread the paint, which must be very diluted, unevenly on the flange of a plate or in the hollows of a relief, then

The illustration below shows a different way of using the level surface of the tile; a plain coloured background is painted, with reserved areas for the motif, which is painted in several colours and shaded. The colours, the drawing and the background must be carefully planned to harmonise with each other.

The stove-tile above, inspired by regional fauna, is of German origin. The background is darker than the pattern, which is naïvely but boldly drawn.

In this frieze of tulips, considerable skill is shown in the variation in colour of the corollas, while keeping the leaves in the lower tiles an identical green. The decorative value of this composition can easily be appreciated.

This Alsatian type of decorated plate is greatly sought after today (right). The dominant colour is a red tinged with purple or brown; a few touches of green and yellow are added here and there. The motifs are slightly different on each piece of the service, but in the same style and colouring.

Traditional peasant patterns are nomadic, as they travel with ease from textiles to wood to faience; with each phase, however, the decorator modifies them and adapts them to suit the material and the object. This faience from Langnau (above) is an excellent example, which could be used as a model.

The Austrian plate on the right serves two purposes, as it combines its habitual usage with that of the ABCs. The border is composed of the letters of the alphabet, which the child will learn to recognise while eating. This plate seems far removed from our commercially produced table china, with its poverty of design.

dab or stipple it, graduating the colour. After firing, this object will still keep its patina when it is washed. Patina applied according to one or the other of these two methods will not only give the object an antique look, but it will soften the crudeness of the decoration and warm the tone of a glaze which is too cold.

Crackling, or crazing, of a glaze is an effect peculiar to faience. This fault may even appear during manufacture, in which case it has probably been caused intentionally. It can also take a hundred years to materialise! Even though crackling gives undoubted charm to faience, it is a great disadvantage in a utilitarian object: dissolved food and dish water can penetrate the porous material through these cracks in the glaze. After a certain time, you will notice a typical and not at all agreeable smell. So if you decide to paint a dinner-service for your own use, choose faience which is free from crackling. The cracks are usually noticeable, but as they are so fine they can be overlooked. Here is a method of detecting them: brush over the object with spirit and if any cracklings exist, they will immediately show up as small stains caused by the spirit having been absorbed by the porous material.

And now—to your paint brushes!

Another example of naïve and successful stylisation is seen in this dish from Simmenthal, Switzerland (above). The flowers are just recognisable as daisies, but the bird, although a bird, is neither blackbird, nor chaffinch, nor robin. It must be remembered that faience decoration does not need photographic accuracy to be successful.

In the age of fancy uniforms, cavaliers even pranced about in the middle of dishes and plates (above). One can of course use these themes which have become folklore; but one could also introduce some aspects of modern life into decorative motifs. The essential is always to coordinate composition, drawing and colour.

◁ Decorating a wall with tiles cannot be carried out without making a preliminary drawing to decide which part of the pattern is to be painted on each tile. This is shown by the illustration on the page left of a fragment of wall from a house in Constantine, Algeria, dating from the beginning of the century.

Traditional flower patterns are very popular. The true artist, however, will not stop there, but will make up designs from favourite flowers and will thus experience the full pleasure to be derived from original creation.

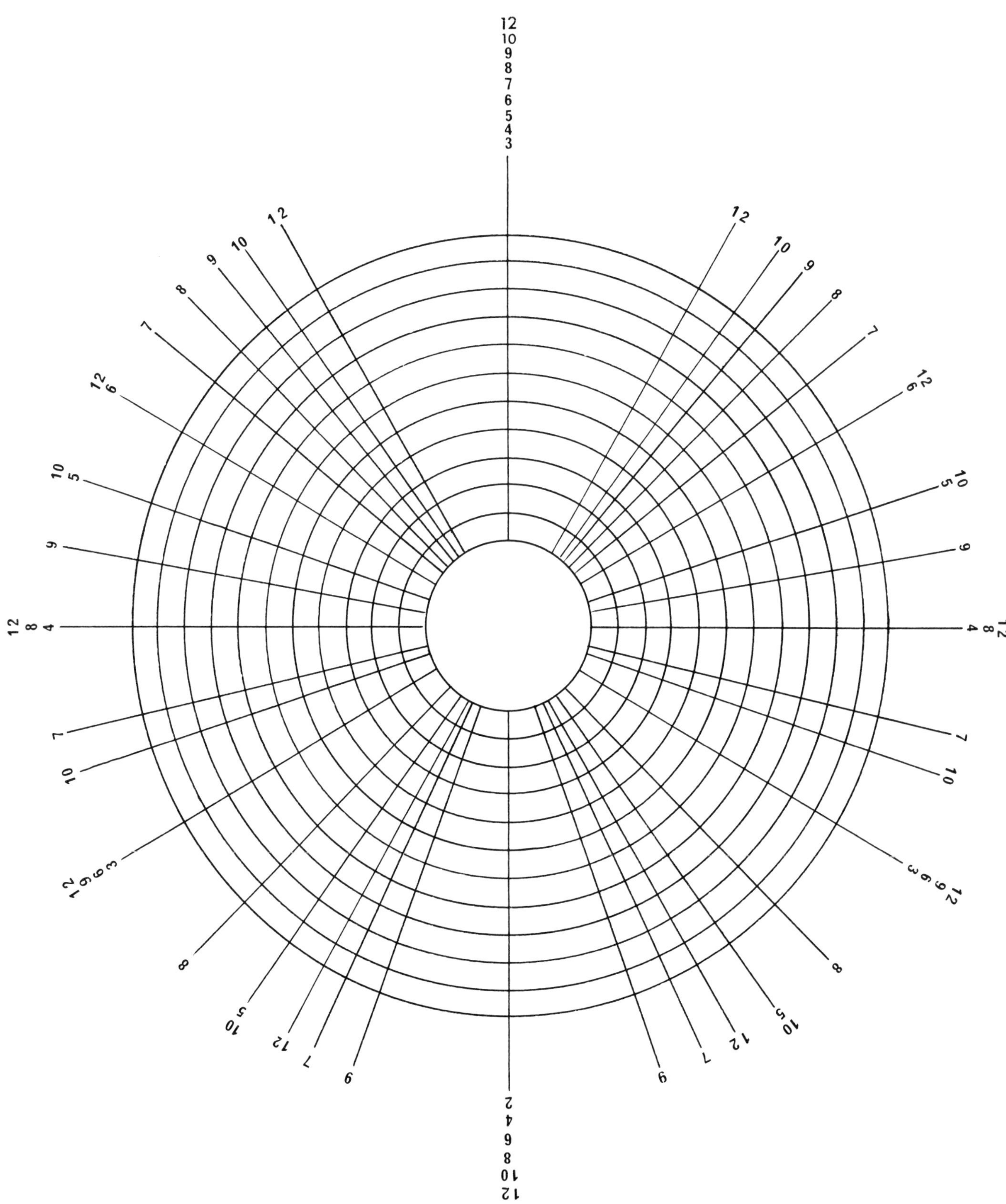

Diagram showing division of a circle into equal parts

NOTES

GLOSSARY

Arabesques: graceful and imaginative ornamentation first used by the Arabs (hence the name) to whom Moslem law forbade the exact reproduction of human beings in the mosques. Arabesques are a mixture of fruit, flowers, real or imaginary animals etc., and were used by the Greeks and Romans, and in Europe mainly during the Renaissance and eighteenth century.

Baldachin, or canopy: baldachin decoration, used in particular in the Rouen factory, consists of pelmet-like hangings in a stiff crenellated shape.

Biscuit ware, or bisque: unglazed porcelain of high quality paste, mostly used for modelling busts and statuettes. Biscuit from Saxony is enamelled, whereas Sèvres biscuit never is, hence the white marble-like appearance of the latter.

Bitumen, Judaean, or Jew's pitch: asphalt extracted from the Dead Sea. Used to protect china from incrustation (or hydrofluoric acid) and to give an antique-looking patina to faience.

Boric, or boracic acid: the name for an acid and an anhydride derived from boron.

Background colour: paint which is applied evenly on an object either by stippling or by immersion.

Burnishing sand: siliceous sand used for burnishing gold.

Cartouches: decorative features used mostly on vases for the purpose of enclosing landscapes or isolated subjects in a framework forming oval or circular compartments.

Cast shadow: the shadow accompanying a decorative feature in order to produce a realistic, trompe-l'œil effect.

Celadon: green china clay which has given its name to certain Chinese ware which, through the centuries, has taken on a whole range of colours—bluish-green, green, pale grey, and bright green with yellowish lights.

Ceramic art: the art of making pottery from the mixing of clay with water, thereby producing a plastic paste which is easy to mould and which becomes hard, solid and durable after firing, producing pottery.

Chatironné decoration: shading, outlining, or hatching made with fine brushstrokes in black or manganese purple. (From the German, *schattieren* —to shade.)

Clay, or potter's clay: natural soft greasy soil. It is practically pure and forms the basis of all ceramic products, and consists of bisilicate of hydrated alumina.

Coiling: also called the 'colombin' technique, is the method of supporting pottery by means of coils of clay arranged in gradually mounting spirals which are afterwards smoothed away and polished.

Cornucopia, or horn of plenty: decoration known as the single or double horn pattern used on Rouen faience, with flowers, fruit and leaves tumbling from a cornucopia. The double horn pattern is also called the truncated horn pattern.

Crackling, or crazing: an effect produced by the splitting of a glaze during firing; used as a form of decoration.

Enamel, see Glaze.

Faience: pottery of porous texture, made from opaque paste and glazed.

Firing: the baking of clay to form pottery, by two methods. First, hard-firing: this describes the period of baking required to harden the paste sufficiently for it to acquire its definitive coloration and for the glaze to melt and the colours to develop. Soft-firing: the period of baking which has the effect of dehydrating the clay and which is usually carried out at temperatures of between 392 and 1,472 degrees Fahrenheit. Pieces are either hard-fired, that is to say decorated on the raw glaze, or soft-fired, when the decoration is applied to baked glaze. The latter process is the safest, the most practical and the least costly.

Flux: a substance consisting of white sand, minium and borax in varying proportions. Mixed with colouring materials it produces enamel or glaze.

Frieze: an ornamental border in the shape of a continuous band.

Glaze: vitrifiable coating which is used to cover pottery. Known as stanniferous or tin-glaze when it contains tin; plumbiferous when containing lead; raw when it has not undergone the firing treatment; and 'fired' when this operation has been carried out. On-glaze (or 'enamel') is painting on already fired glaze, re-firing at a lower temperature.

Grisaille: grey or other subdued colour monochrome decoration of dark tones on light or *vice versa*.

Grained (or 'combed') decoration: parallel lines of hatching tapering to a fine point, similar to the teeth of a comb.

Grotesques: graceful and fantastic decorative designs, consisting of objects and figures mingled with imaginary features.

Impressing: a procedure for shaping objects by means of a plaster mould which is decorated with either a thick or a thin layer of paste either mechanically or by manual pressure.

Inlay: this decoration is carried out by engraving the enamel of the porcelain piece by immersing the object in hydrofluoric acid.

Iron oxide: commonly known as rust. Is found in certain clay soils, forming a natural mineral colourant.

Jaspé decoration: mottled, marbled, striped or blotched.

Kaolin, or china clay: a friable white clay used in the manufacture of porcelain.

Kashmir decoration (generally known as 'Paisley'): a rich medley of flowers and birds with heavily ornamented lambrequins. This decoration, in pseudo-Chinese or Persian style, was mainly used at Delft.

Lattice pattern: a design of interlacing strands or branches resembling large-meshed netting, trellis or basket-work.

Lambrequin decoration: a repeating pattern of pelmet shape, festooned and ornamented with fringes and bobbles.

Lining: the process of decorating an object with one or more lines of varying width from a hair line to a band, in gold or in colour.

Lustre: a shining iridescent coating of very fine consistency usually applied to a fired glaze. When given oxidising treatment lustre resembles the gleam of metal. Lustred pottery is produced by burnishing the clay with a hard implement.

Majolica: famous Italian faience of the fifteenth century. The name is a corruption of Majorca, the island where the art is thought to have originated.

Marli: the raised rim or flange of a plate. It is said to be 'veiled' when it is fluted or buckled.

Matt pottery: pottery in which the clay is left in its natural state, with an unglazed dull surface.

Medallion: a round or oval space reserved on a coloured background or used as a frame to enclose some decorative feature.

Mosaic decoration: an imitation of actual mosaic work.

Muffle furnace: a kiln in which pottery is baked by slow firing in a special internal chamber.

Paste: there are two kinds of porcelain paste; soft paste, an artificial substance which was discovered during the making of successive imitations of hard paste; and hard paste, which is a natural substance based on kaolin, or china clay.

Permanent white: a white which does not alter during firing and which stands out clearly on a background of greyish or bluish white.

Plumbiferous: used to describe matter with a lead content.

Polychrome decoration: decoration in which several colours are used.

Potter's wheel: a kind of revolving table, operated either with the foot or mechanically, for shaping pottery. The lump of clay must revolve so fast that pressure from the potter's fingers is sufficient to cause it to rise and take on a shape.

Porcelain, see Paste: white, waterproof, translucent pottery.

Radiating decoration: an ornamental method much favoured by the Rouen factory, consisting of motifs regularly disposed round the radius of a circle.

Rock-work, or rococo: decoration of capricious, flamboyant, over-elaborate and irregular design, very fashionable in France during the Regency and part of the reign of Louis XV.

Saw-toothed decoration: a cut-out pattern used on the rims of plates.

Sgraffito: a process which results in a decoration standing out against a light background, by using the subterfuge of floating a wash of pale colour on to a dark ground. By then engraving on the pale colour, the dark colour is revealed. The same operation can be carried out in reverse.

Sigillate pottery: to produce this pottery, a process is used which consists of impressing stamps or seals on the wet paste to produce some form of decorative pattern.

Slip, slipware: slip is clay which is either white, or coloured with metal oxides and is either used to mask the colour of the background or as decoration, as found in pottery from Thoune. A transparent glaze is applied finally.

Spring: a fragment of a stem with few leaves, sometimes bearing a few small flowers, as with grasses, cereals etc.

Stanniferous: matter with a tin content, such as tin-glaze.

Stippling: spreading an even coat of paint by means of a special stippling-brush made of skunk hair.

Stoneware: pottery in which the clay is baked at a high temperature and becomes semi-fused, thus acquiring greater hardness.

Terraced decoration: decorative motifs in detached style on a landscape background, such as flowers and birds in 'terraces'.

Terracotta: clay shaped and baked in a kiln, of a rosy colour.

Transfer decoration: obtained by tracing the design instead of painting it directly on the object. This method of decoration originated at Liverpool in the middle of the eighteenth century.

Turntable: a small hand-operated revolving table enabling a small object to be lined or decorated, thus avoiding having to hold it in the hand.

Varnished pottery: pottery which is coated with a transparent coloured varnish.

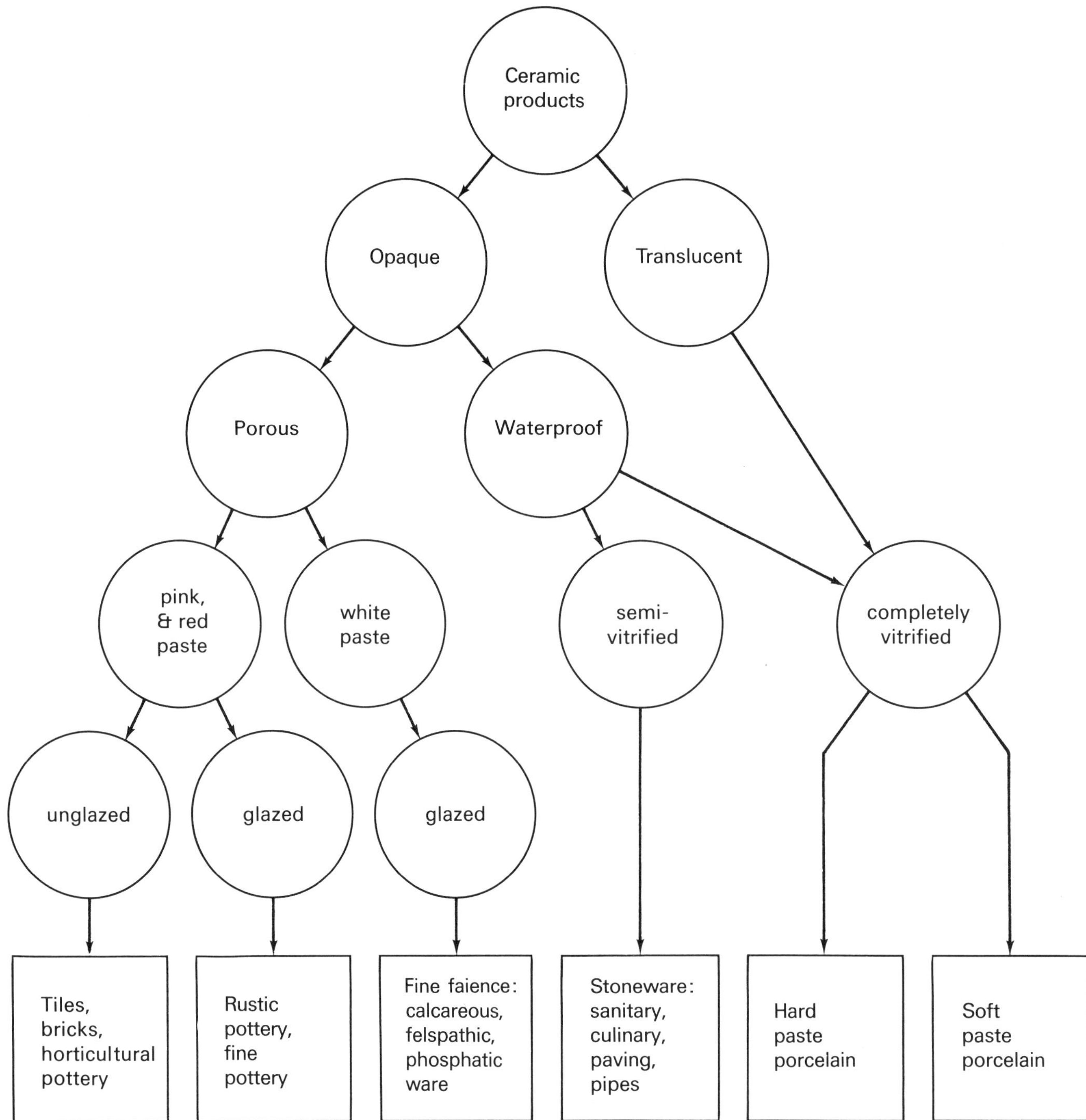

Classification of ceramic products

By studying the conspectus shown above, it will be seen that ceramic products are first of all divided into two groups: opaque products (those which allow no light to filter through), and translucent products. Only porcelain, either hard paste or soft paste, is translucent. The group of opaque ceramics is in turn sub-divided into two categories: products with a porous texture, and those of almost completely waterproof nature (which applies to stoneware and porcelain). As for ceramics with a porous texture (such as white, beige, pink, red, and even black pottery), they present an extremely wide range of products, from the most ordinary such as bricks and tiles by way of rustic pottery and majolica to the most delicate faiences of fine quality such as Wedgwood and Gien. To make for easier understanding, this classification has been drastically simplified; in reality it is much more complex as the dividing line between one substance and another is not so definite. In fact, by a combination of fluxes one can induce certain faiences to acquire the nature of stoneware, and stoneware can develop a degree of translucence.

LIST OF MANUFACTURERS OF UNDECORATED CHINA, ETC.

List of manufacturers of undecorated china

Anita of California
10950 Longford Street
Lakeview Terrace, California 91342
U.S.A.

Arzberg Porzellanfabrik
Arzberg/Oberfranken
Germany

Fürstenberg Porzellanmanufaktur
D–3476 Fürstenberg (Weser) über Höxter
Germany

Porzellanfabrik Hutschenreuther, Lorenz AG
D–8672 Selb
Germany

Porzellanfabrik Thomas am Kulm
D–8585 Speichersdorf, Post Kirchenlaibach
Germany

Staatliche Porzellanmanufaktur Berlin
Wegelystrasse 1
D–1000 Berlin 21
Germany

Porzellanfabrik Langenthal AG
CH–4900 Langenthal
Switzerland

Porcelaines Raynaud & Cie
30, fb. Montjovis
F–87 Limoges
France

Soc. Ceramica Richard-Ginori Spa.
via Goldini 10
Milan
Italy

Royal Worcester China
Worcester House
30, Curzon Street
London W.1
England

Paints most commonly used are supplied by:

Sonie Ames
P.O. Box 1076
Paradise, California 95969
U.S.A.

DEGUSSA
Weissfrauenstrasse 9
D–6000 Frankfurt/Main
Germany

W. C. Heraeus GmbH
Heraeusstrasse 12-14
D–6450 Hanau
Germany

Doris Taylor
715 Fontaine Street
Alexandria, Virginia 22302
U.S.A.

Orders for all material, including undecorated china, paints, brushes, etc., may be addressed to:

Art Consultants
97 St. Marks Place
New York, New York 10009
U.S.A.

Barbara Jones China House
209 W. Niblick
Longview, Texas 75601
U.S.A.

Renaldy's
277 Park Street
Troy, Michigan 48084
U.S.A.

Salyer Publishing Company
3111 N.W. 19th
Oklahoma City, Oklahoma 73107
U.S.A.

Schira Porcelaines
25, rue de Bourg
CH–1000 Lausanne
Switzerland

Messrs. Wengers
Stoke-on-Trent
Staffordshire
England

D. R. Wolfe Overglazes
4165 Barnett Street
Philadelphia, Pennsylvania 19135
U.S.A.

In this book we have not discussed the baking of decorated china. As this requires a great deal of experience, we advise beginners to entrust their work to an experienced ceramicist. For this reason we have not listed the names of any makers of kilns.

CREDITS AND ACKNOWLEDGMENTS

The publisher is very grateful to the following museum curators and collectors who aided in assembling the illustrations for this book:

Abbreviations: t = top; b = bottom; r = right; l = left; m = middle

Ader-Picard-Tajan, Paris/Edita Lausanne: 114 b; Badisches Landesmuseum, Karlsruhe: 97; British Museum, London/Holle Bildarchiv, Baden Baden: 14 tl, m, b; Centraal Museum, Utrecht: 118; Editions Silva, Zürich: 23, 24 b, 106 t; The Hispanic Society of America, New York: 31 t; Historisches Museum, Bern: 17 b, 101, 120 tl; Kunstgewerbe-museum, Köln: 17 tr, 30, 123 mr, b; Metropolitan Museum of Art, New York: 96 b; Yves Millecamps, Paris/Edita Lausanne: 110, 111, 112, 113; Georges Miserez-Schira, Schira Porcelaines, Lausanne/Edita Lausanne: 41, 45, 53, 55, 62, 65, 68, 93, 116, 117, 122; Musée alsacien, Strasbourg: 121; Musée Ariana, Genève: 114 t; Musée des arts décoratifs, Paris/Michel Nahmias-Top Agence, Paris: 90; Musée Cantini, Marseille/ Office du Livre, Fribourg: 19 b; Musée Guimet, Paris 96 t; Musée Guimet, Paris/Photographie Giraudon, Paris: 13 tl, tr, b; Musée Hôtel-Sandelin, Saint-Omer/Office du Livre, Fribourg: 20; Musée du Louvre, Paris/Photographie Giraudon, Paris: 11 tl, b; Musée National de Céramique, Sèvres/R. Lalance, Meudon-la-Forêt: 19 t, 24 t, 87 tr, 88; Musée National de Céramique, Sèvres/ Michel Nahmias-Top Agence, Paris: 89; Musée de porcelaine Richard-Ginori, Florence/Marc Lavrillier-L'Œil, Paris: 28; Museo Civico Archeologico, Bologne: 11 tr; Museum Boymans-van Beuningen, Rotterdam: 119 b; Museum für Kunst und Gewerbe, Hamburg: 26 tb, 27 tb, 84, 86, 91 t, 94, 98, 99, 100, 102, 103, 105, 107, 108, 109; Nordiska Museet, Stockholm: 17 tm; Österreichisches Museum für Volkskunde, Vienna: 17 tl, 120 m; Dr. H. Popta-Gasthuis, Leeuwarden: 21 tl; Rijksmuseum, Amsterdam: 21 tr, 92; Schweizerisches Nationalmuseum, Zürich: 106 b, 123 tl; Victoria and Albert Museum, London: 25, 29, 31 b, 104; Württembergisches Landesmuseum, Stuttgart: 119 tr, m.
The objects on pages 80, 82 t, b, 83, 85, 95 were painted for this book by Marianne Silie.
The models on pages 39, 40, 49, 50, 57, 58, 67, 72 and 73 are from *Cahiers de porcelaines d'Art* Schira, Lausanne.

This book is published under the direction of
AMI GUICHARD
Editorial responsibility and supervision by
URSULA CLAREN
Produced under the direction of WILLY DUBOIS
Printed by the Presses Centrales S.A., Lausanne
Bound by Maurice Busenhart, Lausanne

Printed in Switzerland